COPING WITH MOVING

COPING WITH

Moving

Dorothy Greenwald

THE ROSEN PUBLISHING GROUP, INC./
NEW YORK

Published in 1987 by The Rosen Publishing Group, Inc.
29 East 21st Street, New York, N.Y. 10010

First Edition

Library of Congress Cataloging-in-Publication Data

Greenwald. Dorothy.
    Coping with moving.

    Includes index.
    1. Moving, Household.   I. Title.
TX307.G74   1987   648'.9   87–16558
ISBN 0–8239–0683–3

Manufactured in the United States of America

About the Author

Dorothy Greenwald comes by her knowledge of *Coping with Moving* from hands-on experience. Growing up in Queens, a semisuburban part of New York City, Dorothy had to say good-bye to old friends and learn to make new ones when her parents bought another house a few miles away from the first one. After graduating from Queens College, she moved West to earn a master's degree in English from the University of Michigan.

Her next move took her to the heart of the Big Apple and her very own apartment, a five-story walk-up just off glamorous Madison Avenue. She stayed put for a while, writing feature articles and editing several magazines, including *TV-Radio Mirror* and *Datebook,* a publication for teenagers.

She moved to the West Side of Manhattan when she married Robert Greenwald, a public relations executive, but after they had two children, Liza and Mark, they decided it was time to move on, this time to Montclair, New Jersey.

As a suburban housewife, Dorothy co-authored a book with her husband called *Learning to Live with the Love of Your Life.* When the children were older, she joined Weichert Realtors as a sales associate.

Now on their third Montclair home, they have promised their son, Mark, not to move again—at least not before he finishes high school next year!

Contents

Chapter I

Pity Party or Great Adventure

Moving. It happens to most of us many times in our lives, often at what seems to be the worst possible time. But it's a reality. We're part of a family, and we have to go where the family goes. Moving is what *you* make it. You can be your only guest at a mammoth Pity Party and sit around feeling sorry for yourself. Or—you can accept reality, face it as a young adult, and move on to a new adventure.

Everything Happens to Me!

Bill stamped out of the house and slammed the door. Hard.

"I knew it! I knew it! I just knew things were going too good. I finally make varsity football. The girls stop looking at me as if I'm something that crawled out of a swamp. Even my zits are getting better. And then what happens? Dad has to go and get transferred. To Alabama, no less. I'm not even sure where that is. It's just not fair. No one else has to move. Why me? Why does everything happen to me?"

It's Not the End of the World . . .

Jim sat slumped in his seat in Algebra. Quadratic equations mingled with broken dreams.

"It couldn't happen at a worse time," he thought. "I really had a shot at being captain of the team next year. And we've got such a great thing going. We could be county champs next year. Now it'll never happen. Not for me, anyhow. I'll be lucky if I even *make* the team when we move." He snapped his pencil in two and sighed. "Well, at least I'll try. I'm really pretty good, if I do say so myself."

His face brightened. "Hey, maybe I'll be better than those other guys." He grinned and straightened up in his chair. "Maybe they've never seen real class before." He chuckled at his own humor.

"May we all share the joke, Jim?" Mrs. Degnan's voice cut sharply into his daydream. "Why don't you come up to the board and show us what's so funny about this equation."

Moving is anything you choose to make it. Virtually no one gets through life without something happening to make one ask, "Why me? Why do I have to be the one?" Moving is one of those things. It is the kind of experience you will probably have to face again somewhere along the line. The way you face it now can set a pattern for the rest of your life.

It's a rough deal? You're right. It's rough. But part of the process of growing up is learning to take life as it comes, the downs as well as the ups.

It isn't fair? You're right. It *isn't* fair. But nobody ever said that life *was* fair.

Moving can be a downer, or it can be an adventure. It's all in the way you look at it.

The Optimist and the Pessimist

Once upon a time there were two little boys. They were twins, but they were as different from each other as they could be.

To David the world was a miserable place. Nothing ever seemed to go right for him. He was the original Everything-happens-to-me kid.

Mark saw the world as a place where something exciting and wonderful could happen any minute. And strange as it seemed to David, exciting and wonderful things often did happen to Mark.

Their parents were puzzled. How could twins be so completely opposite from each other? They were both brought up the same way, given the same clothes, toys, and scrupulously equal amounts of attention, cuddling, and discipline. But it was as if the two came from different planets.

Finally the parents decided to take the boys to a psychologist for testing.

The psychologist took David to a room straight out of a Disney movie. A complete set of electric trains whizzed around a scenic track. A stack of blank paper and fresh boxes of crayons, Magic Markers, and watercolors lay on a large table. There were blocks and puzzles and games. There were wind-up toys and a huge rocking horse. It was toy heaven.

"Now, David," said the doctor, "I hope you will enjoy yourself. Feel free to play with anything in this room. I just want you to have a good time. I'll be back shortly." He left the room and closed the door.

Next he took Mark with him to another room. It was a barren space with nothing in it except a huge pile of horse manure in the center of the room. Then, telling Mark he would be back soon, he left that room and closed the door.

About twenty minutes later the psychologist and the parents went in to see David. He was sitting on the floor, sobbing. The electric trains were off the track. The fortress he had constructed from the blocks had fallen down. The rocking horse was lying on its side, and one of the wind-up toys was scooting around the room as if driven by invisible gremlins. Everything had gone wrong for David. The world was still a gloomy place.

Then they went in to see Mark. He was sitting on the floor in the middle of the barren room, throwing armsful of manure up in the air.

"Whee!" he exclaimed. "Whoopee!"

"Mark," asked his puzzled parents, "what are you so excited about?"

Mark threw another armful of manure into the air. "With all this do-do," he explained, "there must be a pony somewhere!"

Look for the Pony

Bill and Jim were like the twins who were so opposite. Both were on the football team. Both had worked hard and achieved status within their school. But Bill assumed that everything he had worked for would turn to dust when he entered a new school. And because of his attitude, he probably foretold his future accurately.

Jim knew that the first thing he would do in the new town was try out for the football team, and that hopefully he would be good enough to make it. He felt he was probably as good as the average player on any high school team—and who could tell? He might be a thousand times better than anyone else in the new school. Maybe he could get to be captain there, too. Maybe he could win a scholarship to college. There could be a pony out there!

Sue had grown up in Edgemont. She loved the town. It was big enough not to be boring, but small enough so that she knew just about everyone in school. She liked school as much as could be expected and was a good student. She was popular and had a number of good friends.

"I really don't want to move," she said one day to her younger sister, Betsy, shortly after they had been told their Dad's new position in the company meant transferring to another branch hundreds of miles away. "But it's a great opportunity for Dad, and I don't see that we have any choice. You know, Mom keeps telling us that growing up is hard, and I'm really beginning to understand what she means."

The two girls sat in glum silence for a while, each thinking about the friends they would be leaving behind and the scary unknown world that waited for them somewhere out there. Sue looked at her little sister and saw tears starting to form.

"You know what, Betsy," she said, "I bet we're going to love Boston. After all, we know everyone in Edgemont. Nothing exciting ever happens here. Boston is full of wonderful things to do, places to see. We can get to the ocean. We can see where they held the Tea Party. And best of all," she said, her hand sweeping around the room the sisters shared, "we can get away from this nursery-rhyme wallpaper. If I never see Mary's little lamb again, it will be too soon."

Betsy giggled and hugged her sister. "Maybe you're right, Susie," she said, "and don't you think it would be fair if this time I had the upper bunk?"

Greg heaved a sigh of relief. Moving? They were actually going to pack this place in? Fantastic! Maybe he could finally be someone else besides Marty Johnson's kid brother. Everywhere he had gone, his whole life, that's what he'd been. The ordinary younger brother of the All-American boy.

"So you're Marty's little brother," they would say. "I hope you will follow in his footsteps."

Marty was the A student, the quarterback who had brought the school its first victory over Bloomfield High in ten years. He had a great voice, and when he played the lead in *Sound of Music* half the girls in the school fell in love.

It made Greg sick. He liked Marty all right, most of the time. He really was a nice guy. But the way everyone seemed to worship him...it made you feel as if you could never measure up. Now he'd have a chance to start over in a place where no one had ever heard of the great Marty Johnson. Maybe now he'd have *his* chance to shine.

Sometimes moving can be the opportunity of a lifetime. Most of us, at one time or another, have wished we could start over. If only I had a chance to do it again, we've said to ourselves, this time I'd do it right. Moving gives you that chance.

Tom's older brother was hardly the school hero. In fact, he had been kicked out of school. All of Tom's teachers were constantly on the lookout for "another problem kid in the family," and many of them were only too willing to point to ordinary misbehavior as evidence of another bad seed. Tom was relieved to move so that he could have a chance to be judged on his own merits—or demerits.

Sam had a learning disability. It had kept him way behind the other kids for many years, but with special help he was beginning to catch up. He was still a slow reader, but his other skills were close to grade level. Sam was as smart as any kid in the class, smarter than some, but he felt like a dummy. Everyone knew he'd been slow, that he'd needed extra help. Now, in a new school, he'd be just like everyone else. Like Tom, Sam looked forward to moving, to having a chance to start over.

The Choice Is Yours

Like it or not, if your family is moving, you are probably going to go with them. You can go kicking and screaming, or you can go off to conquer new worlds. But go you will.

Asking "Why me?" is self-defeating. Things like this just happen. Someone else will get the good teacher, get into the college you had your heart set on, nab the one job that could make your career a success... It happens. Learning to face disappointment and some-times even heartbreak is part of life. The more mature you are, the more easily you can deal with some of the bad times.

And, as Joan Rivers says: "Oh, grow up!"

How to Say Good-bye

Did you ever notice how most people have a hard time saying good-bye, even in an ordinary social situation?

You are visiting Aunt Agnes and Uncle Joe. Family business, gossip, world catastrophes have all been discussed, argued, and put to rest. There's nothing else anyone could possibly say. Cousin Bob takes you into his room to show you his new sixteen-track stereo.

"Time to leave..." your mother calls.

"Can't I stay just another ten minutes," you plead. "Bob has this neat..."

"Absolutely not," says your mother. "Put on your shoes and your coat. This minute!"

So you do. And then you spend the next twenty minutes standing around with your coat on while your mother and father (also with their coats on) talk about all the things they forgot to talk about during dinner.

Finally you leave, but it seems as if the good-bye lasted longer than the visit.

Saying good-bye always seems to be hard. We just don't like to do it. In a social situation we prolong the good-byes—not because we have something so vital to add to the evening's conversation, but because we really don't want to leave our friends. Saying good-bye is much, much harder when you know you may never meet again.

We have all had some kind of saying-good-bye experience...

Maybe it's a best friend from nursery school who moved far away when you were in third grade. You still exchange Christmas cards, and once every few years you see each other when his or her family is traveling north or yours goes south, but sometimes you remember the special closeness the two of you had and wonder if you'll ever have that close a friendship again.

Perhaps it was the friends you made during those fantastic two weeks at summer camp. You may know that you will see each other at the winter reunion and that some of you will be lucky enough to be back in your old bunk next summer, but how are you going to get through that long cold winter without the fun-loving companionship that developed among you?

The most common experience in saying good-bye is going from one school to another. You may have had to leave some really good friends when you entered high school, and there may even have been a teacher who was hard to leave behind.

This time it's even more difficult. This time you are saying good-bye to *everyone* you know—friends, teachers, family—the whole world you have grown up in...people you like, people you love. And you have to face the possibility that you will never see some of them again.

Jane was a lonely kid. She was always the outsider.

She was the last one chosen for the team in Phys. Ed. While the other girls were giggling and throwing Twinkies at the boys during lunch period, Jane sat on the sidelines doing her homework. Came eighth grade and the Senior Prom, and it was a given that Jane would not attend.

Then Jane went to high school, and the ugly duckling turned into a swan. There were new kids to meet, kids who didn't know that Jane was a throwaway and who didn't treat her like an outcast. The curves on her body began going in the right directions, and her face began to show the attractive features that had been hidden by the baby fat.

She started to feel good about herself. She smiled. Her eyes sparkled. She talked with other students. She made some friends. She went to parties. She became part of a group of girls she really liked. One day she woke up and realized she was popular.

That was when her parents told her they would have to move.

Jane was devastated. "How can I leave all my friends?" she sobbed. "I'll never be able to make new friends. I'll be an outsider again. It will be worse than ever, because now I know what it's like to be part of it all..."

Jane really has very little to worry about. She had to learn how to make friends, but she learned her lesson well and she can do it again. That won't make it any easier for her to say good-bye, and she will probably be lonely at first, but the confidence she gained in high school won't disappear when the moving van leaves town. It will stay with her and help her create a similar kind of social life in her new school.

Billy and Sam grew up together. They had been best friends ever since kindergarten. When Sam fell out of a tree and fractured his collarbone, Billy broke his arm trying to break Sam's fall.

When Billy was told that his batting wasn't strong enough to make the baseball team, Sam spent three hours every day after school pitching to him until he was hitting a respectable .265.

They saw each other every day. They shared every secret. They played together, laughed together, and sometimes fought together. Even when things were bad, the world was always a friendlier place because they had each other to talk to, lean on, and let it all hang out with.

Billy would have moved to the end of the earth—gladly—if only Sam could have come with him. But that wasn't the way it was. Billy had to leave, and Sam had to stay behind.

Billy and Sam had an extraordinary friendship. Because it was so deep and true, it may be one of those rare ones that continue to thrive despite the miles, and they may be friends for the rest of their lives. It does happen.

But the real treasure they gave each other is the ability to share. Having discovered the secret of being a real friend, they can build new friendships wherever they are.

I'll Never Love Again

Marie and Tom were in love. They knew it from the minute they crashed into each other on the lunch line.

Somewhere between sponging off the spaghetti that had flown all over Tom's white sweater and picking the pieces of salad out of Marie's long brown hair, their eyes met. It was more like a music video than real life. Without a word they understood that they were meant for each other.

In the two years that followed they were always together—meeting in the hall between classes, going to the library, or studying at each other's homes. Tom was was on the football team, and Marie cheered him through every game—and cheered him up when he needed it. They were the envy of all their friends. Aside from a few occasional explosions, the course of this true love did indeed run smooth.

Then Marie dropped the bomb. She was moving in June. Very far away. The pain they felt was something neither had ever experienced before. They really hurt inside. All the time.

Marie's parents pointed out that if this was really love it would last, that when they were older they could get back together. That only made things worse.

This really was love—here and now—and leaving each other felt like a kind of death. A week before Marie moved, they made a major decision.

They had always fooled around a lot. Everybody did. But they had never "gone all the way." One evening, when Marie's parents were out for a few hours, they consummated their love. It didn't just happen. They planned it.

"We may never see each other again after Monday," said Tom. "At least we'll have this memory."

As it turned out, Marie left with more than a memory. She left carrying Tom's child.

Whether your love is real or just another high school romance, moving creates strong emotions that can be difficult to deal with. You are particularly vulnerable at this time.

You may have very strong convictions about when you want your first sexual encounter to take place. It may be important for you to wait until you are married or are more mature. Don't be embarrassed by these "old-fashioned ideas." They are sound values, and you should stand by your convictions.

But if you feel, as Marie and Tom did, that they wanted their special moment together, make sure that both of you take precautions. Allowing yourself to be swept away may seem romantic, but an unwanted pregnancy is not really a desirable souvenir.

Is It for Real?

When you are in love, the world is beautiful. When you have to move away from the person you love, the world is ugly and full of pain. That's the reality, and no amount of good advice will make it stop hurting.

But there is one important question you should ask yourself, and you owe it to yourself to answer it honestly: "Is this for real? If we stayed together, would it have lasted?"

Very few high school sweethearts get married. If you have to leave the person you love, it's a good time to ask yourself some hard questions. It may ease the pain of leaving—and it will surely teach you something important about yourself.

The True-Love Test

1. *What did I really see in him/her?* Was it really some special inner quality you reacted to in the other person, or was it external—a beautiful face, a great build, the popularity that made you feel popular too, or the prestige of being the boyfriend or girlfriend of a VIP?

2. *Love or habit?* Why are you still together? Is it because you still care deeply for each other, or has it become like wearing old sneakers—comfortable, but going nowhere.

No one feels the same intense kind of emotion in a long-term relationship that you felt in the early days, but if you think you are in love, you should certainly feel *some* intense emotion *sometime*. Do you? Or do you feel it is more like having a brother or sister you don't fight with.

3. *Going steady by default.* It's a security blanket. You don't have to compete on the open market. You have someone to be with at parties, football games, dances. You feel a bit superior to other kids who haven't hooked up with someone. It takes all the anxiety out of your social life. There's nothing wrong with any of that. But just don't kid *yourself* into thinking that it's true love.

4. *Are you secretly glad to be free?* You certainly have warm, loving feelings toward the other person. You will miss him/her intensely when you move away—but sometimes you feel as if he or she is crowding you, always there, never giving you any space. In the midst of heartbreak, you realize you are

thinking about the fun it might be to find someone new...

New Face in Town

The hardest thing about moving is leaving your friends. The scariest is, "Will I make new friends?"

Groups and cliques are already formed. It's one thing to be "in" with kids you've known since you were three. It's another thing to make your way with kids who already have well-established ties with each other.

Is the picture all gloom? Not at all. You have an ace in the hole. *You* are the new kid in town.

Do you remember how annoyed you were last year when all the boys were acting dopey over the blonde with the long eyelashes who appeared in the middle of the term. There was nothing so special about her. But of course there was. She was *new*! And you will be too.

You will be the something special that just blew into town. After nine or ten long years of looking at the same old faces, a fresh one is a treat.

And think how lucky *they* are. Something special has blown into town. You!

Goodbye Is Not Forever

Okay, so NOW you're facing reality. You're moving. You're leaving your friends behind. There's nothing you can do about *that*. But friendships don't *have* to end just because you don't see each other every day.

Friends are too precious to discard. Friendship is

worth the effort. You can keep in touch with friends if you really want to.

How lucky we are that Mr. Bell invented something called the telephone. But—get permission first. Don't spring even an occasional long-distance call on your folks. Ask them about it before you phone and, if you're thinking of the phone as your main tie to your old friends, be prepared to pay for the calls yourself.

Letter-writing is so old-fashioned that it may even be "in" again by now. Sitting down to write a letter once a week is a chore, and once a week will probably turn into once a month and then dwindle down to exchanging Christmas and birthday cards with little notes jotted on them.

Few people today seem to be able to maintain a written correspondence, but there is a way around it. You could keep a daily journal or diary. Just write a few lines each day on some loose-leaf paper, then pop the pages in an envelope at the end of the week and send them off to your special friend.

It's one way to share the emotions, conflicts, joys, and sorrows of your new life. Your friend is the one person who can understand *exactly* how humiliated you felt when you found out that the Benetton you wore to class the first day had been "out" for months, or *exactly* how great you felt when the coach saw you run and commented, "Not bad."

You'll have someone to "talk" to even though you're far apart. It will help ease the pain of separation—and who knows? If you become famous some day, those scribbles of yours could be worth a fortune.

You say letter-writing is a great idea—for someone else. It's just not for you. Then how about talking into a tape recorder and sending the same tape back and forth. Just sit down for five minutes once a week, open your mouth, and see what comes out.

Mail it off to your friends back home and then—hopefully—enjoy five or ten minutes of gab from them as they update you on who's going with whom, how much worse school has become since you left, and why you're the luckiest person in the world because you escaped.

Dig up that old Instamatic or Polaroid that you received for graduation. You used it twice with great enthusiasm and now are not quite sure where you put it.

Send back snapshots of your new world to your friends—your new house, the street you live on, your new school, even your new room when that takes shape. And ask your friends to send you pictures, too, so that you can keep up with what's going on back in your old hometown.

The most ordinary things can have meaning when you're no longer around to share them: pictures of the kids dressed up for Halloween, the Christmas decorations on Main Street, scenes from the school play, the gang in their new spring outfits. They all help you keep in touch and relieve some of the loneliness you are bound to feel.

Unless you actually are moving to the end of the earth—and chances are you're not—you can probably go back and visit your friends from time to time. What's required, however, is some basic *planning*. Wishing won't make it so.

Try to earn some money—and *save it*! Then plan ahead for a visit over a weekend or during school vacation. Ask your friends to visit *you*, and help to make it happen if they're not into advance planning.

Teacher's Pet—or Pet Teacher

Somewhere along the line everyone has a favorite teacher, the one exception to the rule that all teachers are sadistic, sarcastic, and stupid. This teacher was different. He or she had a sense of humor, was friendly, seemed to be a human being, and actually taught you something.

Barbara and her Math teacher, Mrs. Hoffman, were friends. They really liked each other. When Barbara walked into Algebra 103 she was prepared to face her doom. Instead she found a patient, effective teacher who was able to make most algebraic mysteries understandable in class, and who was willing to take all the time in the world after school to work further with any of her students. That's how she and Barbara became friends.

Mrs. Hoffman was more like a big sister than a teacher. She had the kind of sensitivity that allowed Barbara to feel free to cry it all out when her parents grounded her from the Thanksgiving dance because she was failing Spanish.

"That's the easiest language there is," they told her

angrily. "Your problem is you're just lazy. You don't want to work."

But Mrs. Hoffman understood. She knew that some kids just can't deal with a foreign language right away. It takes them longer to catch on. She helped Barbara arrange a conference with guidance people who could explain the problem to her parents.

Even though Barbara had now miraculously passed on to Algebra 203 and no longer had Mrs. Hoffman for a teacher, she still made it a point to stop by her room every few days just to talk. And if things got really rough in the outside world, she knew she had a shoulder to cry on.

When Barbara's folks told her they were moving to another city, her first thought was that she would be losing Mrs. Hoffman.

"What am I going to do without you?" she wailed. "I won't have anyone to talk to..."

"Have more faith in yourself," Mrs. Hoffman said to her. "You've done a lot of growing up since we first met, and you have a lot more strength than you know.

"It may be all for the best. It's time you tried to work out a better relationship with your parents. You can do it if you give yourself a chance. And I'm only a phone call away..."

It's because a special relationship with a teacher is quite rare that it can be particularly hard to leave it behind. Yet the reality is that in a few years you would have to leave that teacher anyhow. Your high school days will end, and the loving, supportive older brother or sister that a teacher has been for you will no longer be a part of your life.

When you enter a new school you may find another teacher you can relate to. You can't count on it, but having formed such a special relationship once, you may be able to do it again. In any event, what you had was something to be treasured. Giving it up is one more inevitable step in the often-painful process we call growing up.

Family Ties

Moving is particularly difficult when you are part of a warm, loving family and your new destination is too far off to make ordinary visits possible. No more eating until you burst at Grandma's Thanksgiving dinner, or Easter egg hunts with all your cousins, or Christmas Day visits to pick up presents from under a dozen different family trees...

You're leaving all that behind, and you've got to know that for all practical purposes it's gone forever.

You can't expect the whole family to pick up and visit you, but you and your family can carefully plan to try to get "back home" occasionally at holiday time. It also helps to know that the old saying, "Blood is thicker than water," is true. Your family will always be your family; no matter how far away you go, you will never lose them.

There are some things you can do to keep close. Try an annual exchange of family portraits. It doesn't have to be elaborate. Ask a friend to take a few Polaroid shots and send them off to the family at Christmas.

Think about a cassette, a video tape, or a home movie. If your little sister is learning to play the violin, let the folks back home share your suffering. If your brother is becoming the hot shot of the basketball team, try to catch some of the action.

Maximize the Minimum

So now there will be just the four or five or six of you, but no matter how large your immediate family, if you left behind aunts, uncles, and cousins by the dozen, you're going to feel all alone.

Make the most of what you have now. If it's a birthday, make sure it's a whale of a birthday, with party hats and balloons and trick candles on the cake. Think about taking time to do more things together as a family. Plan a picnic, a day at the zoo, or even just a trip to the local shopping mall where everyone gets a dollar to splurge on anything from souvlaki to Pac-man.

Create a New Family

Although you will be leaving your real family behind, you can still have family wherever you go. Just build a new one.

You will often meet people who have no family nearby. Most of the time it doesn't matter to them, but it can get awfully lonely at those special times of year.

Comes Thanksgiving, round up the strays. Do you or your parents have friends who will be having dinner all alone in front of a TV set? Ask them to join you. In a few years you'll have such a large "family" you'll have to rent a hall.

Invite friends to share holidays they do not celebrate. Ask a friend of another faith to help you trim the Christmas tree or paint Easter eggs or partake of a

Passover seder. Share your traditions with your new friends and enlarge the circle of good feelings that come with these holidays.

Moving to Maturity

There is one final comfort to keep in mind as you say goodbye to your friends, teachers, and family: Moving today is something that can help you grow up.

Some day you will move again. You will leave home. Perhaps you will be going off to college, or getting married, or moving into your own apartment. Your experience now can help you be better prepared to deal with a more significant move.

Chapter III

Should You Stay Behind?

Dad's being transferred to headquarters in another state. It's the opportunity he has been waiting and working for. But he has to be "on board" in six weeks, and you still have six months until graduation. So where does that leave you?

Opportunity doesn't knock at your convenience. Dad doesn't have to point that out to you, but neither is he pointing the way to a solution that makes sense to you.

"I'm sorry it's happening now," he tells you, "but we have to move. Look, don't worry. We'll work something out for you in your new school so you can graduate on time."

Does that mean you are stuck? That you should simply pack up and move? Not necessarily.

A move like this can be more significant than your parents may realize. Sometimes it can affect the rest of your life. Even if the effect is not that serious, however, it may be important for you to try to work out a way of staying behind until you finish school.

Finding Alternatives

Tom's family found out in July that they would have to move. They were sorry Tom would have to change schools when he had only one more year to go, but they would be settled in their new house in ample time for him to start the next term at his new school. At least he wouldn't have to enter in the middle of the semester. It wasn't ideal, they agreed, but it wouldn't be too bad.

As for basketball and a potential college scholarship . . . Well, certainly Tom was such a good player that he would have no trouble making the team, and college scouts could spot him just as easily at one high school as at another.

"Sorry, folks," said Tom's coach. "It just doesn't work that way."

When the coach heard about Tom's plight, he had suggested stopping by to talk to Tom's parents. Tom was worried about moving, and the coach backed him up.

"Sure, Tom is good," he told them. "Good enough to win an athletic scholarship. *In this school.* But there are no guarantees at another school. He may not make the first team. And if he does, there may be other really strong players who will take the spotlight from him. The coach may not like his style, or—and I know this is hard to believe—he may not like Tom and may not give him the chance he deserves.

"Tom's my boy. He's the best, and anything I can do for him, you know I will. So how do we make it happen?"

Tom's coach and his parents began to talk about alternatives. As much as they would miss him, they agreed it would be best if he could stay behind. But how? They didn't know anyone he could stay with, and they couldn't afford an apartment or a motel for him.

It was Tom's coach who came up with the solution.

"There are lots of big old houses in this town where people rent out rooms on the third floor. I know an older couple that has a house like that. They don't need the money, but they might like the idea of having a strong young man around the house who could mow the lawn and shovel the snow and do all those odd jobs that always crop up."

It was an ideal solution. Tom not only had room and board in exchange for doing chores, but he had a surrogate family to keep him from being too lonesome —and to give his parents the comfort of knowing that someone was taking care of him.

Jennifer had a year and a half to go at Music and Art when her folks told her the bad news. Giving up her friends and a school she liked was bad enough, but they would be moving to a small town where the high school had no special music facilities.

Music had been Jennifer's life from the time she was old enough to climb up onto the piano bench. Her piano playing had won her easy acceptance at the highly competitive high school she now attended. Music was a part of her daily schedule at school, with courses in theory as well as supervised practice. Was she concert caliber? No one was making any promises, but she knew the prize might be hers—if she kept working.

Moving meant giving up all she had worked for. Yes, she could take private piano lessons and practice at home, which she did even now, but she would be outside the music world and might never get back in. Missing a year meant losing momentum that she might never be able to regain.

Her parents were extremely understanding when Jennifer suggested that she stay on to finish school, but they felt she was too young to be on her own in the city. And Jennifer wasn't too sure how she felt about that herself.

Then she had an idea. Just because they were moving didn't mean they had to give up their apartment. Cousin Lisa was about to finish college, and they knew she wanted to get a job in the city. When they had seen each other during spring break, Lisa had said that she hated the idea of moving back in with her parents, but she knew she couldn't afford an apartment of her own. What if she moved in with Jennifer?

They could share expenses. Jennifer had already started giving a few piano lessons to children in the building. With some thought and effort she could get more pupils. Somehow she and Lisa would be able to work it out.

It was a good solution. Jennifer was able to complete school, and her parents felt comfortable about leaving their daughter with a loving, responsible older cousin.

Susan was devastated. She had six months to go until graduation. It was crazy to transfer to a new school for one semester. And if she did, she would be an outsider. She knew it sounded silly, but Senior Prom was something she and her friends had talked about from the time they were freshmen. And then there would be the parties, the overnight at the shore—all the things that were senior traditions.

"You've got to be kidding!" was her dad's comment. "You don't want to move because you want to go to the Senior Prom? That, as you would say, is The Pits!"

Her mother was a bit more understanding, but she too felt that Susan's approach was frivolous and immature. They had to move, and that was that. Susan might as well face it.

But why did she have to move, Susan pleaded. She had it all worked out. She could stay with her friend Melissa, sharing her room. Melissa's parents had already agreed.

It was like talking to a stone. Her parents didn't even want to discuss it. They were a family. They were moving. Susan would move with them. Period.

That Sunday Susan went to church. She wasn't the most regular churchgoer, but today she felt the need. She stopped to talk to the Rev. Montgomery after services, and before she knew what was happening, the story came rushing out. To her surprise he didn't laugh at her or tell her she was silly to want to stay on at school.

"Would you like me to talk to your parents?" he asked. "Perhaps I might be able to help them understand your point of view."

Susan felt as if someone had given her a great gift. That evening the Rev. Montgomery stopped by at Susan's house. He spoke to her parents about things called emotional needs and somehow made them see how important these next six months would be for Susan. By the time he left, Susan had received permission to stay with Melissa, and her parents had a new insight into their daughter.

Children's Rights

Tom, Jennifer, and Susan were able to work out solutions to their problems. Their parents understood that they had a right to stay behind when the family moved because of the special hardships the move would create. There are times when it is in the child's best interest to stay behind. It is certainly the right of any child to discuss this with his or her parents and to ask some vital questions:

1. *Can the move be postponed?* It's written in stone: You have to move *now*. Probably true. But if you have only a short time left before school ends, isn't it worth asking if the move can be postponed?

If your dad explains the situation to his supervisor, the likely answer will be: "That's too bad, but we need you at headquarters now, not six months from now." But isn't it worth asking?

It is just possible that the move is not all that urgent, that with some judicious travel and groundwork, the actual move could be put off until you have completed school.

2. *Can the family stay behind?* The transfer is inevitable. One of your parents has to move to another city or town in order to keep a job or move up in one. Is there a possibility that that parent could go ahead while the other parent stays behind with the rest of the family? Sometimes this is an answer that makes sense, as difficult as it may be for your parents. Again, you have the right to ask that question if you believe it is essential for your well-being.

3. *Can you stay behind?* Tom, Jennifer, and Susan solved their problems by staying behind. Tom found room and board with a family in exchange for doing household chores. Jennifer kept the family apartment and gave piano lessons to help pay her share of the

expenses. Susan simply moved in with her best friend. But there are as many other solutions as there are situations that arise.

One road is to take a job as a mother's helper in exchange for room and board and usually even a small salary.

If baby-sitting and supper dishes are not your bag, perhaps you can earn enough money during the summer or on weekends and evenings to pay for a room, or a share of one, in a private home. Many families rent out a room when their children leave home.

A local Y may be an answer to a place to stay. If it costs more to stay there than your part-time jobs cover, perhaps you can arrange a loan from your parents to pay the balance.

Then there are always assorted friends and relatives, or perhaps a combination of them. A month with Uncle Joe and Aunt Martha, another month with your friend Bob or Doris, and then back to Uncle Joe and Aunt Martha. That way, none of them will get too fed up with you, and you'll still be on good terms with all of those nice folks when you leave.

Parents Have Feelings, Too

Before coming on like Dolby sound and making pronouncements about the rights of adolescents, do remember that parents are people, too. They have feelings—and those feelings can be hurt.

You believe it will be too disruptive if you do not finish out the year at school. You tell your parents so, but it comes out all wrong. They end up feeling that the only reason you want to stay behind is to get away from them. That's not the case (at least it isn't the main reason), but they seem to feel it is.

Tell them how it really is. Don't *assume* that they will understand that your need to finish school is the reason you want to stay behind—and that they know you're not using it as an excuse to get away from them. It's important to say the words, to make sure that you do not hurt them unintentionally.

How to Find Help

You've done everything you can. You've come up with a full assortment of ideas that would enable you to stay behind, and still your parents say no. And what's more, they don't want to hear another word out of you on the subject.

What to do? It's time to turn to someone else for help.

Susan spoke to her minister. He was sympathetic, and her parents respected him. They listened to what he had to say.

The key is right there. The person who can help you not only has to understand your position but has to be someone your parents respect.

Perhaps you can turn to a teacher, a guidance counselor, or even the principal of your school. If sports are involved, your coach would be a natural ally, as Tom's was. A religious adviser or family doctor could be helpful, since they are used to dealing with family problems in the course of their professions. Sometimes an old family friend or relative can see things in perspective when your parents can not.

A Lesson in Life

Standing up for what you believe, expressing your needs in loving terms to your parents is also a growing-up process. If you can convince them that your viewpoint is right and get them to go along with you, you will have taken a major step toward control of your own life.

Chapter IV

Up-Front Help

Moving is one of the most traumatic situations you will ever face in life. Only death, divorce, and marriage cause more anxiety or stress. Anything you can do to relieve the stress of moving will make you feel better about what lies ahead.

Knowledge is power. The more you know about a new world you are about to enter, the more comfortable you will be in it. Before taking a trip to a foreign country, a seasoned traveler searches out every bit of information available on the area. The country will still be strange, but because the traveler is familiar with some of its customs, geography, and history, he or she will be more relaxed, more able to enjoy the new experience.

When you have to move, the greatest favor you can do yourself is to learn beforehand as much as you can about the new area. It may be far away, a place you have never even heard of. It may be just across town. But even then, in many ways it will be like traveling to a foreign land.

Cross-town or Cross-country

Sometimes the move is voluntary. Your parents decide they want a different house—larger or smaller, newer or older. More land (Wow! room for basketball practice!). Less land (Hey! less lawn to mow!). More closet space, more bathrooms, more bedrooms (*A room of your own!*). A better kitchen, a nicer neighborhood, a prettier street.

The good part of this kind of move is that it is usually not too far away from where you now live. It may be just across town or to a nearby town. Chances are you will still be able to see some of your old friends from time to time. But even when you are not facing the pain of total separation, you will still be a stranger in your new day-to-day world.

When you move, it usually means going to a new school. Sometimes the move is because your parents want you to go to a different school—smaller classes, a wider choice of courses, better teachers. Even when it's "for your own good," it's rough to start over again in a ιew school.

It's even rougher to start over again when *everything* is new. Moving is not always voluntary. Relocation has become a major industry because so many people are constantly being transferred from one part of the country to another. Military transfers have always been common, and corporate transfers are on the rise. It can be very scary to know that tomorrow you will wake up in a strange room, in a town you have never seen before, and where you don't have a single friend.

Research and Resources

Knowing some facts about your new school or your new town won't make *all* those bad dreams go away, but it can help a lot. You have been learning research skills from the moment you trooped down to the school library in first grade. Those skills can pay off now.

Learning about your new school is the first step on the road to feeling comfortable there. But before you can learn about it, you have to know which school it is. As dumb as it sounds, many young people don't even know the name of the school they will be attending when they move, much less the first thing about it. You can check that out with the real estate broker or relocation service that may be handling your move, or you can contact the local Board of Education.

Visit your new school if at all possible. Call or write to set up an appointment to talk to a guidance counselor and the principal. (The principal! Why *not* the principal? His or her attitude may tell you more about the school than any other single thing.)

Prepare a list of questions, and don't be embarrassed to refer to it. Some starters might be:

1. Will you get credit for all the courses you have taken so far?

2. If there is any problem with credits, can you make them up in summer school?

3. What class will you be in? How many students in a class?

4. Do they offer courses in your special interest: music, art, drama, computers?

5. How about sports? What do they offer, and how do you join the team?

6. What about other after-school activities? Clubs? Publications? Service groups? Sororities? Fraternities?

Ask for a copy of the course catalogue, the school handbook, the school newspaper, and any other publications. Ask for a tour of the school. Visit a classroom, the lunchroom, the library, the gym, any special-interest areas: a computer center, the weight room, the art or music studio. Try to talk to a rep from the student council.

Spend some unofficial time in the school after the tour is over. Talk to some of the students. How do they like the school? What are its pluses and minuses? Are the kids friendly? Do cliques set the pace? What are some of the values here? Is scholarship prized or scorned? Do clothes make the student? You may not like all the answers you get, but at least you'll be prepared for some of the realities ahead of you.

A personal visit is, of course, the best way to learn about your new school. Obviously, that isn't always possible. In that case, you can write for some of the basic information: the catalogue of courses, the student handbook, and any student publications. Then, if you have any questions, you can always call the guidance department or school office.

Talk of the Town

Although school is your Number One Priority, you will also feel much more comfortable about the move if you know something about the town or city you are moving to. Again, a visit is the best bet. There is no substitute for physically driving up to your new house, looking the neighborhood over, talking to some of your neighbors. Even the little kid scooting by on his tricycle can give you a feeling for the street.

But even if you are lucky enough to be able to visit your new home, there are a few things you should do that will be as helpful to you as they are to the person who cannot make the trip.

The very best way to learn about a town is to subscribe to the local newsaper. The Chamber of Commerce can give you the name(s). Smaller towns usually have only one paper, and that one may serve several towns or the entire region. Some cities have more than one paper. Send for sample copies, and subscribe to the one that seems to carry the most local news. That may not be the best one, or the one you will buy after you move, but it can best serve your needs now.

The local Chamber of Commerce provides many services besides telling everyone what a "great town we have here." Call or write and ask them to send you suitable material. It usually has local street maps, calendars of special events, and pamphlets about how the town is run or nearby places of interest. If you are moving to a large city, indicate what part of town you will be living in so that the C of C can zero in on your particular needs.

You should also ask if the town has a Welcome Wagon. That is a volunteer service that gathers together all sorts of material about a town and calls on newcomers to explain what's what. Do take advantage of it if it exists. Welcome Wagon not only tells you everything you need to know, but the packet usually includes discount coupons from various merchants in town.

Hit the Books

So you haven't been back to the library since Miss Winchell drove you and the rest of the seventh graders there with a bullwhip. You're gonna be very surprised. The library has these neat little packages called books, and some of them can open your eyes about your new world.

To start with, there are travel guides to every part of this country. Some of them contain extensive information that can help you get a feeling for your new home. They talk about climate, history, natural wonders, commerce, industry. They list special sights to see, good places to eat, local festivals and fairs. (If your folks belong to AAA or another travel club, you should also contact them for this kind of material.)

Talk to the librarian. Tell her where you are going and ask what books or magazines she might suggest. Novels have been written about virtually every part of our country. *Growing Up in Foggy Bottom* may not win the National Book Award, but if you're moving to Foggy Bottom it can be a treasure. There are also many regional magazines. For example, *Yankee* is a periodical that covers the New England area. *Arizona Highways* is famous for its spectacular photographs of—you guessed it.

Your Business Is Their Business

Did your family buy or rent through a real estate broker? Use their facilities to the fullest. Ask them to gather information for you on your new town and to give you the name of an associate in the area. If the relocation service where your mom or dad works is making the arrangements, help can easily be obtained from the new office, and the people who work there are usually more than willing to help a newcomer get settled. If the move is long-distance, the moving companies often have basic information.

Follow the Faith

One of the major networks in the country is the religious group to which you belong. You can ask your pastor for information about a similar or compatible church or temple. He may even volunteer to contact a colleague in another area—and you can be sure the welcome mat will be rolled out.

Check Out the Club Scene

Do you belong to the Scouts, YMCA, American Youth Hostels, 4-H—any large organization that might have members in other parts of the country? Turn to them for help. Ask for names of people to contact... nearest location of groups...someone of your own age you could write to. It's great to know there will be at least one friendly face in town.

The Old Boy (Girl) Network

Talk up the move in school. Spread the word as to where you are going. You may find the network working for you. Your English teacher has a colleague in your new school. She will send her a note. When you are a bewildered new student trying to cope with a confusing world, it can be great to have someone to turn to—even an English teacher.

Friends of friends, of course, are the best. They can help you over the roughest part—when you feel all alone—and they are a link to those you left behind. If you are lucky enough to have that kind of contact, use it. The girl your best friend went to camp with when she was eleven may not turn out to be a subsitute for your best friend, but she can help you over the hump.

Help Yourself

You can arrive in your new home bewildered and befuddled, or you can arrive with a fairly good idea of what to expect. The choice is yours. It takes a little time and planning, but it pays to help yourself.

Chapter **V**

The Heat Is On

Sue looked at the glum faces around the dinner table. Her father hadn't said a word since he sat down. Her mother asked if the soup was hot enough, and that was her contribution to the evening's conversation. Her little sister, Betsy, was splashing her spoon gently in the soup, staring at the ripples she was creating. The only sound was a loud slurping from her older brother, Tod, whose head was about one inch from his bowl.

"Do you always have to make so much noise when you eat?" Sue asked irritably.

"Listen to Little Miss Perfect," Tod snapped.

"Sue's right, Tod," said Mrs. Benson. "Your table manners have been going straight down the drain lately."

Tod slammed down his fist. "Why doesn't everybody just get off my back!"

"Don't you speak to your mother that way!" Mr. Benson commanded. "If you can't behave like a human being, you can leave the table."

"That suits me just fine," shouted Tod, pushing back his chair and stomping out of the room.

The Bensons finished dinner in silence.

"What in the world is happening to us?" Sue asked herself. "It's like we're falling apart."

Parents Have Problems, Too

Dinnertime at the Benson house used to be a noisy, friendly time of day, a time when they swapped experiences, opinions, gossip. If someone was having a problem it usually surfaced before dessert was finished. Solutions were freely offered—and some of them were even helpful.

When Mr. Benson said he was being transferred to Boston, Sue was able to make her peace with the move. Although she would have preferred to stay in Edgemont where the world was warm and familiar, she was excited about moving and the great variety life in a big city could offer.

Having made her peace with the move, and actually anticipating it now that the time was coming closer, it never occurred to Sue that other people in the family might still have serious problems.

Her father, usually patient and understanding, was more on edge every day. Boston was the Big Time for his company. That was where you went when you made it—and if you didn't continue to make it once you were there, it was a long way down.

Sure, he knew he had the qualifications for top management. That was why he had been selected for the new job. But what if...

It was the "What ifs" that got to him. What if his judgment was wrong? What if he was really getting in over his head? There was no turning back now. What if he had made the wrong decision...?

He had little patience for the warfare between Sue and Tod. He was sorry he had lost his temper, but he found it harder and harder these days to put up with what seemed to be contant bickering. He was anxious to make the move and find out what the future really held for him. Until that was settled, there was no way he could truly relax.

When it comes to stress, moving is right up there at the top of the list. Even under the best of circumstances, it is one of life's most difficult challenges. Psychological studies indicate that moving ranks third when it comes to producing anxiety. Only death and marriage (or divorce) create more stress than moving.

Your parents usually have a lot more at stake than you do—and you certainly have enough on *your* plate. Most young people do not want to move. Who wants to go from the familiar and comfortable into a strange new world? Even if you hate your school, even if you look upon moving as a chance to start over, that doesn't mean it's a comfortable thing to do.

You may be moving because, like Mr. Benson, your father or your mother has been transferred to a new position in the company, or to another military post. The best of all possible worlds is when the move is made because a better job is in the offing. And yet, even with that, stress is normal because your mother or father is facing a test—and life offers no guarantees.

Although it is no longer uncommon for moving to revolve around a woman's career, most job transfers today still take place because of a man's work situation. However, since more and more women are now working to supplement the family income, they usually have to start all over again when their husbands are transferred.

A few companies have begun to offer job placement for wives, but in most cases the wife has to start job-hunting all over again. She has probably worked very hard to get where she is today. It will certainly be frustrating to give up all she has accomplished.

So Mrs. Benson is just as concerned—and worried—over the decision to move as Mr. Benson is. Will her skills transfer? Is she getting too old for the job market? Will she be able to cope with the pace of working in a large city?

Mrs. Benson is also under stress. Even if she and Mr. Benson were to decide that the increase in salary was large enough so that she would no longer have to work if she did not want to, she would still feel stress because she shares her husband's concern about his new job.

Sometimes the picture is a bleak one. Your father or mother may have lost the job he or she had and there may be no suitable jobs around. Often we have to move to another part of the country to go where the work is. Certainly you can imagine the kind of stress your parents would face at such a time.

Even though your father or mother may have lost a job through no fault of their own—perhaps because a plant closed down or a company went out of business—he or she may feel defeated by having to move to another area to find work. Such internal pressure may make them absolutely impossible to live with.

It may seem to you that they are behaving unreasonably—and they probably arc. There is very little you can do about it except to be aware of the causes of their irritability, to try your best not to provoke them, and to be as understanding as you can. After all, you will admit that you have not always been the easiest person to get along with. Chances are your parents have done more than their share of stepping softly with you and trying to understand this peculiar creature called a teenager.

Just as you will find it hard to leave your friends, your school, and the world you know, so will your parents. They may be leaving behind all the people they grew up with, or friends they have made over the years. It may mean breaking family ties, being far from their parents, brothers, sisters and all the warmth and support a family gives.

Your parents may be active in town. They may belong to groups where they love to work and enjoy the companionship that has been built up over the years. They may have a regular bridge game going, or play poker every week. They may be important in the structure of the town, involved in local politics, president of the PTA, coach of Little League.

It will be hard for them to leave all that behind, to wonder if they will find the same kind of opportunity in their new surroundings, and that, too, will create stress.

Little Ones—Big Troubles

Parents and teenagers are not the only people in the family who will have problems with moving. If you have younger brothers or sisters, they will certainly feel the strain as well. The younger they are, the more bewildering and frightening it can be.

In spite of the daily squabbles, in spite of the times you would gladly have sold your little brother to the first used-child dealer that came along, chances are that somewhere deep in your stony heart is a small spot of affection for "that brat." Your parents may be so pre-occupied with their own problems that they are not aware of the devastating effect the whole situation may have on a little one.

When the Johnsons moved, Mr. Johnson's company took care of everything, helping them find a new house, hiring movers, packing up the house. It made life *almost* pleasant.

Two days before they were due to move, three huge men descended on the Johnson house. Swiftly, methodically, and with great expertise, they began to pack everything in sight. They started on the main floor and worked their way up.

Mrs. Johnson supervised the packing with four-year-old Marilyn constantly at her side. At last they came to Marilyn's room. She watched with growing wonder, her eyes getting larger and larger, as everything, except the tattered bunny she clutched tightly in her arms, was packed away. Before long the room was bare.

"What next?" one of the burly men asked.

Marilyn flung her arms around her mother's legs and started to sob. "Don't let them pack me, Mommy," she howled. "Don't let them pack me!"

It's Not My Problem!

So your kid sister is having nightmares, your father is shouting at everybody, and your mother bursts into tears when you ask her to pass the salt. So what does that have to do with you? It's not your problem. You didn't create this mess.

You're right. You didn't create the problem, but you *may* have some responsibility to help your family cope better with what's going on. Look at it this way:

Everyone is getting into everyone else's hair. You are the one person who realizes that last week's full moon did not cause the whole family to be transformed into beasts. You know it's the pressure of moving. And you know in your heart that with that knowledge comes responsibility. You'd like it all to go away, but it won't. So what can you do about it?

Solution #1: Be an ostrich. You can wish very hard that it will all go away. Or you can try to make yourself invisible so that no one will dump on you. You can convince yourself that there's nothing you can do anyway, so why try?

Solution #2: Face reality. You can face the facts and meet them head-on. You might, for example, try to talk things out one night at the dinner table, or, if your family is never in one place at the same time, actually call a family conference.

You might begin by pointing out that everyone has probably noticed a change in the atmosphere. You're all so irritable, you make problems out of situations that you would have previously ignored. Everyone is getting into everyone else's hair.

Enough, you can say. Let's all calm down and realize that we are under stress because we're moving. Can't we try to be more patient and understanding with each other?

We all love each other, you can point out. The family won't break up because we're fighting more than we usually do. It will pass. But wouldn't be great if we could make a real effort to help each other right now? Isn't that what families are for?

Try to get each member of the family to talk about

how he or she feels, the angers, the fears, the way they feel others should behave toward them.

Whatever the words you want to say or whatever means you use to get the family together to hear them, you can be of great help to the people you love by exercising leadership right now. It won't take the stress out of moving, but it will help each of you deal better with the inevitable pressure you must feel at this time.

Chapter VI

PLAN AHEA
D

Rosemary didn't want to move. She hated everything about it. She wouldn't talk about it, plan for it, even think about it. Maybe if she ignored it, it would go away. She knew what the reality was, but she preferred to avoid reality until it caught up with her.

When the time came to pack, she tossed everything she owned into unmarked boxes, barrels, suitcases, and trunks. She stuffed last-minute leftovers into her knapsack and stormed out of the house.

She arrived at the new house, weary, tear-stained, and absolutely unfit for any of the tasks that lay ahead. When the moving men asked where she wanted her bed or desk or dresser, she didn't know, so they set up her room in the way that was most convenient for them.

Her clothes, books, records, and tapes were scattered all over the house. A carton of books was found under the dining-room table. Her winter clothes were finally unearthed in the garage. Her tapes were missing for months. It wasn't until she heard "Meaty, Beaty, Big and Bouncy" coming from her brother Tom's room that she discovered what had happened to her collection.

Rosemary knew she would hate this move and *everything* about it—and she was determined to prove her point. Moving was indeed Pity Party time for her, and not the Great Adventure it could have been.

A Creative Caper

You may look on yourself as plodding, uncreative. Art and design are for the other guy. You were turned off when your second-grade teacher made everyone draw Mexican sombreros and you got a D because one side of the brim was twice as wide as the other. Now you're getting a second chance. You can design your new room. It's creative. It's fun to do. And best of all, it's easy.

Maybe you're lucky enough to be getting a room of your own, but even if you're sharing it, somebody should decide where the furniture looks best, what color the walls should be, how to decorate the room.

If it's your own room, no problem. You make the decisions. If you are sharing, talk it through with your brother(s) or sister(s). Everyone should have their say in designing the new room—if they want to. It saves lots of grief later on.

Decisions, Decisions

Decision #1: Do you want to design a new room, or do you want to duplicate your old room? If you are perfectly happy with the way things are and don't want to bother creating a new arrangement, leave it alone. Don't mess with perfection. But at least work out a floor plan so *you won't have to start moving furniture all over again* after the movers have left.

Decision #2: Do you want to keep all your old things—the Humpty Dumpty lamp, the Snoopy bedspread, the furry pink rug with the indelible Coke stains? You love them. Moving to your new house with these comfortable old things is like taking along a security blanket. Obviously, don't change a thing. But if the thought of something new or a bit more sophisticated turns you on, see if you can work it out.

Ask your folks if there's room in the budget for a few new things, or help pay for them by disposing of the oldies in a garage sale.

A tasteful, inexpensive item can bring a little zip into your new room. It might be a museum poster or a bright red beanbag chair. Those architect-type desk lamps come in great primary colors and give great light to work by. How about a set of black-and-white striped sheets—something that really makes a statement.

Decision #3: What colors would you like to use in your new room? You may have lived all your life with pink roses on the wallpaper or brown cows jumping over the moon.

It would be great if you liked whatever is already on the walls of your new room, but chances are you won't. So think color. Would I feel good waking up in a bright yellow room? Maybe sky blue is more "me"— and then there's always basic black. (Only kidding, Mom.)

Unless you're exceptionally handy, stay away from wallpaper. The little old lady the Sunday supplement shows hanging paper with her hat on is probably the publisher's mother and the only thing she ever hung was a picture of her son. Stick to paint. Any klutz can deal with a paintbrush and washable latex paint.

Your Own Space

If you have a chance to visit your new house or apartment, it will be easier to figure out how to set up your new space. Take along pencil, pad, and tape measure.

Sketch the room, making sure you show where the windows, doors, radiators, electrical outlets, and closets are. Make the dimensions as accurate as possible. Measure the complete width and length first. That will give you the floor area so you can determine whether that furry pink rug that you've decided to keep after all will fit.

Next, go around the room from point to point, measuring and observing carefully. How wide is the wall between the radiator and the window? How far is the windowsill from the floor? How high is the ceiling? Is there a light fixture in the ceiling? On the wall? Is there an outlet handy for a bed or desk lamp? What color are the walls? Wallpaper or paint? Could you live with what's there, or does it *really* have to go?

Finally, take some pictures of the room. They will help you remember any points your sketches may not show too clearly. Start at one point in the room and snap it from overlapping angles so that by the time you have taken four or five pictures you have a complete circle.

If you live too far away to visit your new house, try to get this information from someone else. After all, *someone* saw the house. Maybe it was the real estate agent or your father. Ask them to take pictures for you and to give you a plan of your room, or at least a rough sketch.

Very often the people who are selling the house already have all this information. They may have taken measurements when they moved in or would be glad to accommodate you now.

After you have all your measurements, put them down on a piece of graph paper. Try to get some with fairly large squares.

Allow two squares to a foot. (If you're lucky enough to have a very large room, tape two or more pieces of paper together.) Then, with a ruler and pencil, translate the dimensions of your new room to paper.

Now measure the furnishings you will be taking with you—bed, dresser, desk, chair, rug, dressing table, etc. Take another piece of graph paper and outline each piece—again using two squares to make a foot. Then cut out your works of art and *play*.

If you have a rug, put that down first on the diagram you made of the room and then start placing the furniture. When you have an arrangement you think you like, put a piece of double-stick tape on the back of each piece and tape it in place. That permits you to pick up any piece and change its position.

Whether it's your own room or one you share, planning a space of your own is exciting. Go to the library and look at the home furnishings magazines. They are full of great ideas that you can adapt to your new room.

Check out the handyman books. They show step-by-step plans for building everything from bookshelves to bunk beds. (Just a hint: a dozen bricks and some boards equal a low instant bookcase. And hanging standards and brackets for shelves isn't all that hard.)

Designing your own room now can serve you well all

your life. And an extra added bonus—the activity of designing the room and the anticipation of what your new space will look like takes some of the heaviness out of moving. You are not simply going away from something. You are moving *to* something.

And Don't Forget...

In the midst of this burst of creativity, don't overlook some of the most essential practical things:

1. Transfer records. Stop in at the school office and ask them to send a transcript of your record to your new school. Try to do this early on, so that your transition from one school to another will go more smoothly.

Ask your doctor and dentist for a copy of your records, or, if you know names in advance, ask them to send your records directly to the new doctor or dentist.

2. Change of address. Be sure to give as much advance notice as you can to magazine publishers or you will miss some issues of your favorite magazine before it catches up with you.

The Post Office has little packets of cards for Change of Address. They are also handy to give to friends or send to people you correspond with.

3. Pamper your pet. Whether your pet is a goldfish, a hamster, or a pedigreed poodle, special arrangements *must* be made for moving day. Even if the move is local, you still should figure out the best place for your pet while everything is in chaos.

Perhaps you can park Fido with a friend for the day. Move your gerbil village to a safe spot—away from the moving men—so it won't end up on the van sandwiched between the sofa and the piano.

If your move involves public transportation, be sure to check with your vet and see what he recommends. Also check with the carrier to find out their requirements. (Can your pet go on the plane or train with you, or must it travel separately?)

Planning Pays Off

Planning makes the difference between complete chaos and comparative calm. Murphy's Law (Anything that can go wrong will) is still in effect, but you don't have to surrender to it completely. Take charge of your life. Use your capabilities and intelligence to work for YOU.

Chapter **VII**

Clean Up Your Act

Your closet is packed so tight you can't squeeze an empty hanger into it. Your dresser drawers are overflowing with shirts you wouldn't be caught dead in, jeans you outgrew two years ago, and pajamas you've had since you were ten. You don't have a thing to wear! Well, maybe one or two things...

One of the great advantages of moving is that it creates an opportunity for you to clean up your act—to weed out the junk, to take a fresh look at what you own, to end up with the wonderful feeling of being in control of your own things instead of being overwhelmed by them.

Many well-dressed men and women have comparatively limited wardrobes. They shop carefully, buying the best clothes they can afford. They sacrifice quantity for quality, knowing that if they buy something that is well made and is becoming to them, they will always feel good in it.

Take advantage of the move to look carefully at your clothes and decide which you want to take with you. Spend some time actually trying on everything in your wardrobe—and be ruthless about it.

Does that pale green sweater make you look as if you had spent the night dancing on tombstones? Could two of you fit in the painter's pants you bought last summer? Have you always hated that nice navy blue skirt your mother picked up on sale?

Ask yourself some questions:

Does it fit?
Is it becoming?
Do I like it?
Will I wear it?

If the answer to any of the above is "No," don't take it with you. Put it aside for the moment.

My Favorite Things

We all have things we could never bear to part with: the teddy bear that lost its eyes, ears, and one leg so long ago...the flattened football you once scored a touchdown with...a faded party hat...a well-worn copy of *Little House on the Prairie*...

There is no reason to leave your treasures behind just because you are moving. Memories are made of things like that. But oh, the junk we collect and keep simply because it's there.

Take a hard look at your toys, games, stuffed animals, books, records, tapes. How long has it been since you last played Candyland or listened to Uncle Remus tell stories about Bre'r Rabbit? Do you really need *all* the notebooks you've had since first grade? Do you want that giant stuffed tiger to take up his half of your new room too?

Put aside the things you have outgrown, don't want,

don't like, and separate them from those things you do want to take with you.

Interior Decorating

Finally, look at the furniture in your room and the pictures, posters, and pinups that adorn the walls. You now have a floor plan of your new room. Will all of your old furniture fit? And even if it does, do you want to take all of it with you? Do you need more room for books or records? Does Kermit the Frog still light up your life, or would you prefer a Bruce Springsteen poster?

Think about how you would like your room to look. Cool and quiet—or full of life? Try to visualize how the things you have will look in a new setting and what you should do to help them adapt. If something will be completely out of place—and you can buy or make a substitute—leave the old friend behind.

Traveling Money

What to do with that good navy blue skirt, thirty stuffed animals, and the Humpty Dumpty lamp? Hold a garage or tag sale. It's another fun thing to do, and you're bound to make *some* money.

Try to get the entire family to join you in the project. Friends and neighbors are also fair game. Virtually everyone has a white elephant or two they would love to dispose of. The bigger and more varied your sale, the more people it will attract, the more money you will make.

Brazenly tempt reluctant siblings with visions of

extra pocket money. Remind Mom and Dad that every old table, set of dishes, or shelf of books they leave behind is one piece less to move—and one less carton to unpack.

Urge them to be selective about what to take and what to leave behind, to cull out the dead wood and try to sell it. (Old Garage Sale adage: One person's junk is another person's treasure.)

Do Your Homework

Start making the rounds of local garage or tag sales as soon as you make the decision to have one of your own. Look for items similar to those you will be selling and make notes.

The secret of any sucessful sale is pricing right for the market. After stopping in at half a dozen sales for three or four weeks, you will get a feeling of how to price things at your sale.

Pay special attention to the way a sale is set up. Grade it on how it appealed to you. Did it make you want to buy—or turn you off? Are certain things usually placed up front to atract the buyer? What can you learn from someone else?

Buy a supply of tags, stickers, marking pens, and oak tag for signs. Give some to everyone in the family and have each person start to mark his or her own things.

Use a different color tag or marking pen for each person. It will make it easier to keep track of how the profits should be divided. After each piece is marked, put it in a place designated as garage-sale storage.

Discuss the most convenient place to set up the

sale—garage, porch, lawn, driveway, or inside the house. Think about the best way to display your merchandise based on your observation of other sales.

Check out local custom and usage. Do you need a permit to hold a sale? Can you just post signs? Is there a hometown paper where you can place an inexpensive ad? Pay close attention to what other people do. If you spot a good ad, one you find particularly attractive, try to follow it.

Be sure to use the words "Moving Sale" in your ad and your signs. It has more appeal than the ordinary garage sale because it suggests not just old junk that people want to get rid of, but more interesting pieces that won't fit in a new home.

Boost your sale with words like "Exceptional!" "Giant!" "Three Generations!" "Five Family!"— assuming the statements are true, of course.

If you don't want to advertise, signs alone are quite effective. Put them up—loud and clear—on the nearest busy streets. Include your address and the time and day of sale.

You might want to run the sale for two or three days. You will probably sell less each day, but once you have gone to the trouble of setting up the sale, it doesn't take much more effort to extend it. If the sale is outdoors, get some rolls of clear plastic sheeting to cover your tables at night or in case of rain.

Getting the word out is vital. Use every means at your disposal. If you do, indeed, have a wide variety of items to sell, make sure you get that point across.

Be specific in your advertising and try to highlight things you think will be specially appealing. (Boy's 24″ bike—like new; wicker rocker; Victorian plant stand;

redwood picnic table w/benches.) If you are selling lots of clothes, books, records, and toys, be sure to mention the fact. Many people do much of their basic shopping this way.

Traveling On

The sale is over. You feel ten pounds lighter and, hopefully, your pocket is jingling. Don't be disappointed if you don't sell everything. That's almost impossible. Gather up the left overs and dispatch them to a local charity. It will make you feel good, and if you keep a list of what you are giving away, Mom and Dad may get a tax deduction.

Chapter VIII

A Survival Kit

The average family moves once every five years. This may be the first time you have moved, or you may already have moved two or three times. It is never a lot of fun. At best it is tolerable. It can be a nightmare, but it doesn't have to be. Surviving moving day is a skill that can be learned.

A Family Affair

At times of stress a show of support within the family can make all the difference. Your mom and dad have been there for *you* when you needed them, and chances are that even your rotten kid brother and impossible older sister have been amazingly supportive when it really mattered.

Moving matters. If every person in your family carries his or her own load, no one is overburdened. Even fairly young children can pack their own things and help with the general move. It may be only dusting off books or putting plastic containers in a carton, but it's an important job.

Every little bit really helps. It's not only the right thing to do, but when your family is involved in something as significant as moving, it feels good to be a part of it, to know you were needed and did your share.

Packing: Winners and Losers

Packing is not hard, but it takes time to do properly and it requires thought. It is a skill that, once learned, you can call on for the rest of your life. You can meet the challenge head-on and conquer it, or you can let it overwhelm you and go down to defeat.

Marjorie felt the walls closing in her. The word was out: We move in three weeks. Start packing up your room NOW.

"How am I ever going to deal with all this junk? I don't know where to start," she wailed.

The task seemed more than she could handle. Paralysis set in. She did nothing. Then as Moving Day grew closer and closer she panicked and started flinging things into cartons.

Her collection of delicate glass figures—carelessly wrapped—was tossed in with her shoes just to fill a carton. It arrived, not surprisingly, in pieces, and she mourned it like a lost friend. It took her weeks to find her other pair of sneakers because she didn't mark any of her cartons. Moving to a new town was hard enough, but Marjorie created problems and tensions that didn't have to be there.

Kevin was miserable when he found out the family had to move. He didn't want to leave his friends. Life could sure be unfair sometimes. The only good thing about moving was the packing.

"You're off your bird," commented his friend Jason when Kevin shared this weird confidence. "Packing is the pits. I should know. We've moved three times in the last eight years!"

But packing was a comfort to Kevin. For one thing, it kept him busy every spare moment so that there was less time for self-pity. But the truth was he really did enjoy it. He liked going through the box of old junk that he had accumlated over the years. Sorting out what to keep and what to toss brought back people and events that had once been important in his life.

Never known for his neatness, Kevin discovered that he got a kick out of pulling stuff out from under the bed—his second closet. (So that's where that softball went!...I always wondered what happened to my green swim trunks...Wow! My Led Zeppelin tape!)

Bit by bit Kevin went through his possessions, packing slowly and carefully, surprised at the satisfaction he got out of marking and sealing a carton. As the cartons mounted up one by one in his room, he felt better and better about the task of moving. After all, it wasn't getting *him* down. If he could deal with this, he could deal with tougher situations and handle them well.

Packing: First Aid

Any move has three aspects:

1. Decisions and confusion—before the movers descend...

2. Agony—while they toss your precious possessions into those mammoth caves they call vans...

3. Numbness—after they have been paid and you are all alone to face what they have wrought.

You can survive—and conquer—all these demons with a little training in First Aid. Basic equipment includes cartons, tubes, tape, rope, markers, labels, lots of old newspapers (start saving right now!), and the answers to a few important questions.

What to Do Before the Movers Come

1. Check the moving company to find out if it supplies cartons or if you must scrounge for yourself. Generally speaking, movers do not include cartons in their original estimate of costs. They will gladly sell them to you, but if you need a lot, it can become expensive.

Sometimes they will sell you used cartons (in decent enough condition) for a fraction of the price of a new carton. You can also pick up cartons free from your local market or liquor store. Stop by and ask when they put their cartons out and whether you can help yourself.

You may want to suggest that your folks invest in some of the heavyweight cartons called "dish barrels." Once upon a time these were actual barrels, but now they are just heavier cartons that give more protection to delicate objects.

Movers usually provide large flat cartons for mirrors, so if you have one in your room, make sure they know the size. If you have posters you want to take with you, ask about tubes that you can roll the poster into for safekeeping.

2. Inquire about wardrobes. Usually they are included and are delivered the morning of the move or the night before. They sound fancy, but they are usually just tall cartons with a bar across the top for hangers. The great advantage is that you can transfer your hanging clothes from your closet directly to a wardrobe, saving many steps of packing and unpacking.

Shoes, boots, belts, and ties can also be packed directly into a wardrobe. Shoes and boots would, of course, go in first, down at the bottom, and belts can be tossed in over them. Ties should be secured on a hanger with a crossbar. The simplest way is to knot the tie loosely around the crossbar.

3. Find out if you can leave your dresser and desk drawers intact. Impossible as it sounds, that is usually permitted. You probably will not have to empty the drawers. On moving day the movers will wrap your dresser or desk in a huge padded blanket, secure it with ropes, hoist it on the back of the strongest mover (there is always one who can carry *anything*), and send him staggering to the truck.

The Self-help Route

Not everyone hires movers to do the moving. Depending on the size of your move and the number of willing backs you can round up to carry things, you can hire a you-haul-it van, truck, or carrier.

It makes the packing harder because, unless your friends or family are built like Arnold Schwarzeneger, you will probably have to empty all drawers. Wardrobes will most likely not be included in your plans because they are fairly expensive, so everything in your closet must go into cartons.

But you can certainly save a bundle by going the self-help route. And there's a very special feeling that comes from doing a difficult job with a little help from your friends.

The Order of Things

Where do I begin? Don't throw up your hands in despair. It's really as easy as A, B, C.

A. Anything you don't really need. Your collection of miniature mice, all those pictures of David Bowie you cut out from magazines and stuck up with Scotch tape on your walls, your class pictures from nursery school on, a zoo of stuffed animals—any things you really don't need all the time (no matter how much you like them) should be the first things to be packed. They are the hallmark of your room, they give it personality. But you have to start packing somewhere, and that's a pretty good place.

Begin with the breakables. Take a carton and a bunch of old newspapers and go to work—carefully. Put a layer of newspaper on the bottom of the carton. Wrap each piece individually in as much paper as it takes to make it feel well padded. Put crumpled paper between items so they will be secure and not go bumping into each other. Fill the top of the carton with more crumpled paper. If you have room left on top, you can put in very light objects such as a sun hat or lampshade.

Give the carton a number (this would be #1) and write the contents on the outside ("Mice, tan lampshade"). Start a master list to tell you that Carton #1 holds your rare mice collection and the tan lampshade.

Take everything off the walls—pictures, posters, and pinups—and pack them away. If there is glass in a picture frame, pad the front with newspaper, then wrap with more paper and tape it in place.

To protect the glass further, stand pictures on end in the carton, not lying flat. That is also good advice when packing dishes. Don't stack plates on top of each other; stand them up on end.

Roll your posters and slide them into tubes. One tube can hold many posters if they are rolled snugly. Identify the contents, even though you're positive you will remember where you put what. Six weeks later, when you're searching for your Rolling Stones poster, you'll be happy you scribbled the name on the tube.

B. Books, records, and games. The best part of this category is that it's easy to pack, but, unlike Category A, some decisions are involved here. Special books like a dictionary or other reference books have to be set aside for last-minute packing. That fat paperback novel you bought last summer and never got around to reading might be a good moving day companion.

If you can't live without your album of "Sgt. Pepper's Lonely Hearts Club Band," there's no reason why you should. Keep it out for last-minute packing. You'll find enough other records, games, toys, photo albums, and scrapbooks to empty most of your shelves.

Try to stack books neatly so they fit without sliding around. Stuff newspaper in the empty places. One caution: Use the smaller cartons for books. Remember, a human being has to pick them up and carry them.

Records should, of course, stand on end in a box, not flat on top of each other.

This is also the time to pack as many of your toilet articles and cosmetics as you can. If you have a mini-drugstore set up in the bathroom, consider whether you can possibly struggle through the next three weeks without four kinds of face soap, three deodorants, and twelve shades of nail polish.

C. Clothes. At first glance Category C would seem to be the most troublesome. In reality, if the moving company supplies wardrobes and allows you to leave your clothing in drawers, it's not such a hard job.

Start with the seasons. If it's winter, you know for sure you're not going to have much use for your bikinis, tank tops, or white shorts. And if it's summer, chances are you can get through the next few weeks without three wool pullovers, two flannel shirts, and a pair of heavyweight jeans.

Since clothing is light, use your largest cartons here. If you like the wrinkled look, just dump your clothes into cartons and enjoy; but if you prefer a neater image, take a little time to fold and place things carefully.

Work your way through the seasons until you narrow your wardrobe down to clothes you might possibly want to use between packing time and moving day.

If you can't decide whether you want to wear something, don't pack it. If you can't decide whether you want to keep something or try to sell it at your tag sale, keep it. Don't try to fine-tune this particular activity any more than necessary, or you'll drive yourself crazy.

Now set aside three large cartons and relax. It takes

very little time to fill a carton with clothes, so you can wait until a few days before you move to pack the clothes you kept out.

Everything you've kept out for possible use during the interim period goes in the first of these—including dirty laundry. (Good idea to put that in a plastic bag to keep it separate from the rest and identify it for washing.)

Pack the second carton the day before you move. This one is for those books, clothes, jewelry, shoes, cosmetics, and drugs that you needed to keep out until the last minute.

There are bound to be other items you forgot to pack—that bulky sweater you didn't notice on the top shelf of your closet, the boots Mother found in the basement, the denim jacket your friend Max just remembered to return. . . . These also go into the second carton.

The last carton is vital to maintain your sanity in moving. It should be marked with red crayon, gold stars, bright green tape—anything that will make it stand out in a crowd.

What goes in here is everything you will need for your first night in your new home. Some of this can be packed well in advance—towels, sheets, pajamas. Other things can be packed the morning of moving day—your pillow and blankets, slippers, bathrobe, toilet articles, cosmetics.

Clothes you would like to wear the first day in your new home should also be in this carton and can easily be packed ahead of time. And don't forget Teddy or Snoopy or that lamb with one ear that cuddles with you at night. That may be the most necessary of all!

Color Me Purple

Anything you can do to identify your possessions when they finally arrive in your new home will make life that much easier for you. Here are a few simple hints:

1. Color-code destinations. Large (2 × 3) self-stick labels are available in a wide variety of colors from yellow, red, and blue to chartreuse and flaming orange.

Each floor in your new home can be assigned a different color label: blue for the basement, white for the main floor, yellow for the second floor. (Don't forget the garage, front porch, and backyard.) If you are moving to an apartment, a different color can be assigned to each room.

Every carton should have a label color-coded to the floor or room it is going to. If you have more than one floor to deal with, every room should have a number.

For example, on the first floor the living room would be #1, the dining room #2, the kitchen #3, and so on. If you decide on white labels for the first floor, then a carton with a #3 on a white label would be headed for the kitchen. If red is to be the second-floor color, cartons marked with #2 on red labels might be going to your room.

A diagram of your new home must be made and given to the moving men. It should tell them what colors are assigned to each floor and how the rooms are numbered.

It also helps to make signs for each room, indicating color and number, that you can post prominently for the moving men to see. A lot of cartons will still end up in wrong rooms, but at least this method gives you a fighting chance.

2. Mark each carton. Besides a color-coded label, each carton should be clearly marked with a heavy marking pen indicating its contents *and* the name of the room it is going to. This may seem like unnecessary work since you already have a label on the carton to indicate destination, but anything you can do to make it easier for the movers to put things where they belong is one for your side. (Besides, labels can come off.)

Keep your own master list of every carton you pack. Yes, you can always look on the side of the carton, but when there are ten cartons piled up in your room, it helps to know just by looking at your list that your sweaters are in carton #4 and your records in carton #2. It's a lot easier than moving each carton to find the side you wrote on.

The Big Day

Moving is the closest most of us ever get to complete chaos. Just assume that Murphy's Law applies. If you are lucky, you will have pleasant movers who will try to do their job efficiently and quickly. If you are not so lucky—well, why borrow trouble?

Just know that the unexpected is likely to happen, that things will get lost, get broken, fall apart.

In spite of labels, color coding, and constant super-vision (an absolute necessity!), your stereo can still end up in the kitchen and you may be tripping over your brother's weight-lifting equipment for the next two weeks. (I'll get it out of your room this afternoon. I promise.)

Roll with the punches. And remember, by nightfall (well, at least by dawn) it will all be over.

Marcia woke with a start. Where was she? Clutching her raggedy Raggedy Ann, she peered over a wall of cartons. By the dim light from the hall she could see another bed with her younger sister, Beth, curled in a ball like a cat, sleeping soundly.

Marcia reached for her bathrobe at the foot of the bed where she always kept it. There it was. Old Faithful. Comforting to find at least one thing where it belonged.

She inched her way past the cartons to the hall. Which way was the bathroom? It was very confusing, not to mention spooky. Fifteen was too old to be scared of the dark, she kept telling herself.

"Are you okay, honey?" Dad's voice was like a bright light, a warm blanket, a hug.

"I'm fine," she said, snuggling into his arms. "I was just trying to find the bathroom."

"Exactly what I had in mind," he laughed, walking down the hall with her. He opened a door and turned on the light. "Ladies first," he said, bowing.

Marcia gave him a kiss and went into the bathroom. What was there to be scared of? Nothing at all. She hoped Beth wouldn't wake up and be afraid of the unfamiliar setting. Poor little kid...

Settling In

The good thing about unpacking is that there's no deadline. If you don't unpack a carton today, you can do it tomorrow—or the next day—or next week.

The bad thing about unpacking is that you have to do it some time—have to decide where to put things so that you can find them again.

The best thing about unpacking is that when it's over you can have the fun of decorating—of creating a new atmosphere, a reflection of the new You.

Try to unpack and unclutter your room as quickly as you can. If everything doesn't end up in The Perfect Place, you can always move it. If you forget where you put your beach sandals, they'll turn up eventually. If the interesting arrangement you worked out for your furniture proves to be a disaster, let it be. You can move things around after you're settled.

The nicest thing you can do for yourself is to turn your room into a mini-oasis. Everywhere else in the house you can expect long-term confusion. It can take weeks for the shelves to go up in the living room, for the good dishes to make their way from carton to china closet. The family stereo may not be set up until just before Christmas. Of course you'll help once you have done some essential unpacking of your own, but be prepared to live with a big mess for a while.

Your room, however, doesn't have to be a big mess. Compared to the rest of the work ahead, your job is limited. If you unpack quickly and get most of the cartons out of your way, you can begin to lead a normal life.

You'll have a quiet place to study, a snug haven for listening to music, a peaceful room where you can relax and find added strength to make your way in your new world.

Chapter IX

Your New School

The first thing you have to face—the biggest hurdle—is your new school. What will it really be like?

Will it be easy or tough? Will the students be friendly or give you the cold shoulder? And as for the teachers...you'd rather not even think about *them*.

Stranger in Town

It happens in Westerns all the time. The good guy on the white horse rides into town. The streets are deserted. He has the feeling he is being watched from behind closed curtains in second-floor windows. He hitches his horse to the rail in front of the general store, adjusts his ten-gallon hat at a jaunty angle, and marches into the store, hoping his confident stride masks the anxiety he feels.

"Mornin'," he calls cheerfully to the sullen young woman behind the counter.

She stares at him, then slowly, deliberately, turns away.

The camera moves in for a closeup of his bewildered face. What's going on in this town? Has he done something wrong? Has he broken some rule he didn't even know existed?

From out of a dark corner an unshaven, disheveled man shuffles up.

"Stranger," he mutters in a whiskey-hoarse voice, "if I was you I'd get right back on that horse and just keep goin'...."

* * *

Dan sat straight up in bed, his palms wet, his fists clenched. A fantasy? Of course. But could there be an element of truth in the fantasy? He didn't think he would be met with open hostility in his new school, but would he be made to feel like the outsider he was? He didn't expect anyone to take him by the hand and introduce him as the greatest thing to hit town since the last Elton John concert, but it would be nice if someone said "Hello."

Over the Rainbow

Laurie wanted to go right back to sleep—and back into the wonderful dream she had been having. It was just like when Dorothy landed in Oz and walked out the door to find the whole town cheering because her house had landed on the Wicked Witch.

Laurie dreamt she was in gym class in her new school.

"I'm desperate," the teacher was saying. "We've just *got* to have someone who can ice skate. It's only two months to the countywide contest. Isn't there anyone in this town who can turn a decent figure eight?"

Shyly Laurie raised her hand. "I'd be glad to try," she said quietly.

Magically the shiny wood gym floor turned to glass-smooth ice, and Laurie's baggy shorts and dirty sneakers were transformed into a sleek royal blue outfit that outlined her new curves. The music began and she was out on the ice, skating better than she had ever skated before—even in her dreams. When the number was over there was wild applause.

"O-kay!" exclaimed the gym teacher. "We've got us a champion!"

* * *

Reluctantly Laurie pulled herself out of bed. Of course it was silly, but the dream made her feel less apprehensive about her first day of school. Maybe it wouldn't be so bad after all...

Fantasies and Fears

Being a stranger is never easy. Virtually everyone experiences some anxiety in the face of the unknown. There is no sure way to predict how people will behave toward you, but if you think about how you felt when someone new entered your school, you will realize that you should expect neither the worst nor the best.

Unless he/she was so gorgeous that it was love—or hate—at first sight, you probably felt pretty neutral about a stranger. You weren't prepared to hoist the newcomer on your shoulders and march him or her around the cafeteria, but you certainly didn't want to run him/her out of town at first sight.

If you're naturally compassionate and considerate, maybe you went out of your way to make a stranger feel at home. If you're more reserved, you waited to see how he or she shaped up.

That's pretty much what you can expect when *you're* the new kid on the block. Your first day probably won't measure up to any fantasies you may have had, but it will probably not be anywhere near the disaster you feared.

School Smarts

Your classmates are only a small part of the new world you enter when you move. The school itself will certainly be different from the one you went to before.

No two schools are alike. Standards and curricula vary widely. You may have moved from an easy school to a more demanding one. Even though you always complained about how overworked you were, you may soon realize that you didn't begin to know what hard was.

Linda was never what you would call a "brain," but she had always managed an easy B. She was determined, now that she was in a new school, to do better, to work hard and to turn the B into a B+ or even an A.

She didn't know what hit her. Two weeks into the new term and she was swamped with work. She tried to keep up but found herself falling behind. So much more seemed to be expected of her. Forget the easy B. It was a struggle to get a C.

It helps if you understand what's happening. Linda didn't have a sudden loss of brain power. It was the school that was different. If it happens to you, don't be ashamed to ask for help.

Most teachers will gladly stay after school for a while or come in early to work with a student who is seriously trying to make it. If extra help from a teacher is still not enough, get a tutor.

Many schools have honor students who are willing to give one or two hours a week (sometimes free, sometimes for a small fee) to a classmate who needs help. There are almost always teachers who will tutor after school. The department office, or the main office, usually has a list of tutors and can probably give you an idea of their fees.

Susan was a serious student. She had always worked hard to maintain a B average. Suddenly she found herself pulling straight A's.

"The kids here are so dumb!" she confided when she called her old friend, Nancy. "I don't have to do any more work than I did before, but I'm getting honors. I don't mean to brag, but I think I'm the smartest kid in the class."

She and Nancy giggled over that one.

"You sure struck it lucky," Nancy groaned. "You should see what they're piling on us this year."

Susan struck it lucky, but not smart. Her attitude began to show. She bragged about how much harder her old school was. She was patronizing to her new classmates. She talked about how easy it was to get good grades in a "school like this."

And she wondered why she couldn't make friends...

You could also strike it lucky. You could suddenly find you're getting much better grades in your new school. Don't let it go to your head.

You didn't have an overnight genius brain implant. It's just that you, like Susan, are in a less demanding school.

You can lean back and spend your afternoons watching the soaps and your evenings on the phone, or you can make the most of your luck. If you're planning to go on to college, a 4.0 average and a top 10 class rank is impressive, even if the new school is not rated quite as high as the one you came from.

But no matter what your future plans are, play it cool. No one wants a friend who (not so) secretly looks down on him or her, or who is always letting you know how great she or he is. You can get some ego satisfaction out of bragging about your brains, but your ego can be lonesome company on a Saturday night.

Teacher Trauma

Vic was worried about his new teachers. He had heard they were really tough in this school.

"Watch your step," he was told. "Once they get on your case, you've had it!"

Vic watched his step very carefully. At the end of the first week he made his own evaluation.

His Math teacher, Mr. Haddon, must once have been a Marine drill sergeant. If school policy permitted, Vic felt sure he would have demanded fifty pushups for each infraction.

An infraction to Mr. Haddon could be anything from coming in late, to a sloppy paper, to falling asleep in class. Fortunately for the students, the worst punishment he could inflict was keeping you after school.

Mademoiselle Minton, his French teacher, was a free spirit. She loved everything French and wanted her students to enjoy learning the language. She showed slides of Paris, taught the class how to make a real French omelette, and even made a game out of conjugating verbs.

The other teachers were somewhere in between boring and better-than-average. Some were strict, others were not. Some were demanding and harsh, others understanding and patient.

They were, Vic decided, for the most part, pretty much like every other set of teachers he had ever had.

Teachers are probably the most stable element of your new world. Of course they have to follow school policy, but there are always different interpretations of the same rule. Most teachers are up there because they love to teach. And that, more than any regional difference, is the common factor.

You will learn from the good teacher no matter what school you attend. If you are seriously interested in learning, you will probably get along with any teacher anywhere. If you're trying to get by with as little effort as possible, you will probably find teachers a constant problem.

"Why don't they get off my back," Sam complained. "I thought they might be different in my new school, but I guess they're the same everywhere. Never satisfied—no matter how hard you try.

Sam isn't interested in learning. He's in school because he has to be there. His attitude shows. He complains about how much work is dumped on him, but he does as little as possible. His greatest effort goes into seeing how much he can get away with.

Teachers are soon disenchanted with Sam. They're

human, too! If a student makes it apparent that he would rather be anywhere but in class, most teachers will be tougher with that student than with a poorer student who is really trying.

"I was scared stiff," said Vic. He sighed with relief. "I heard they would be different here, but I guess they're the same everywhere."

Teachers *are* the same everywhere. So are students.

Once you get past the surface—a regional accent, a gloss of sophistication, unfamiliar ideas—you will find that they are not much different from the students and teachers you left behind.

Just walk in—and be yourself! Before you know it, you won't be a stranger in town any more.

Chapter **X**

Your New Hometown

You did your homework well. You read up on your new hometown before you moved. You found bits and pieces of history in travel books. The county map you sent for showed you what part of town your house was located in and what were some of the sites folks were proud of. The local paper gave you a feeling of what the people were like—their values, their politics, their priorities.

But it's still not the same as actually living there. It is essential to recognize that there can be major changes in your life simply because you now live in a different kind of town. And it is vital that you learn to deal with these changes in a way that will make your transition to your new hometown easier.

City Mouse, Country Mouse

If you live in a small town and are moving to another small town, or if you live in a big city and are moving to another big city, you can strike that adjustment off your list. But if you are shifting from city to country or vice versa, you have some serious culture shock in store.

Do you remember reading this story when you were

little—or having Mom or Dad read something like it to you?

Once upon a time there were two mouse cousins. One lived in the city; the other lived in the country.

One day the city mouse invited his cousin to visit him. He wanted to show him how exciting life was in the big city.

The country mouse almost had a nervous breakdown. The noise, the traffic, the roar of the buses terrified him. His city cousin laughed at his fears.

"A little noise can't hurt you," he sneered. "But dig the pace, the excitement! This is where it's at, man!"

The country mouse hated being cooped up in a world where everything was made of stone—the houses, the sidewalks, the street. It was all so cold and hard, with very few trees and almost no grass.

"But the eating's great," enthused his city cousin. "Living in an apartment house is like going to a different restaurant every night."

The country mouse tried to adjust, but after a while he became very homesick and asked his cousin to come and visit him.

"Dullsville," commented the city mouse. "Who wants to go spend time in a hick town?"

But because he really liked his cousin, and because he was just a little bit curious, he went.

The city mouse almost had a nervous breakdown.

There was this huge black cat, and every time he turned a corner it seemed to be waiting for him.

"Solomon keeps me on my toes," said the country mouse when his cousin complained. "He keeps my wits sharp. He makes life a challenge. He keeps me young."

The city mouse couldn't understand why so much valuable land was being wasted on trees and grass.

"Just fill your lungs with that good air," enthused his cousin.

"I think I'm allergic to the country," said the city mouse, sneezing, and with that he packed his bag and hopped the first bus back to town.

It's a Jungle Out Three!

Steve grew up on a farm. He rode a pony when he was two and learned to milk cows when he was three. He knew everyone in his school and every neighbor for miles around. He grew tomatoes and corn in his own garden and went to the eighth grade dance with the girl next door. (Next door was about half a mile down the road.)

Then the bad times came. Banks started calling in loans and neighbors started losing their farms.

Steve's family held out a lot longer than most, but one day Steve stood with his father, mother, and two sisters in the back of a somber crowd watching Mr. Crowley auction off everything they owned. It was the first time Steve had ever seen his father cry.

Steve's family was luckier than most. His dad had a degree in agriculture from a big university and was a recognized authority on farm management. Despite his reverses, the university thought enough of him to offer him a teaching job. It meant moving to a big Midwestern city. Steve was scared to death.

He had read the papers. He had heard the stories about muggings and worse. So had his mother.

"It's a jungle out there," she protested. "That's where the animals are. Not here on the farm."

Most people who move from the country or suburbs to a big city are apprehensive. Like Steve, they have heard the horror stories, and a lot of them are true. But the fact is that millions of people live peaceful lives in big cities. And they love city life.

Big cities attract people because they offer so much that is not available in smaller communities: great museums, concerts, movies, live theater, unusual restaurants, huge department stores and tiny boutiques. There's a lot to be said for life in the fast lane. There is an exciting beat to a big city, and it is one that young people in particular respond to.

People who live in big cities develop "street smarts." They quickly learn which streets to travel and which ones to stay away from. They learn about avoiding eye contact with certain people. They learn about putting money in a shoe. They learn about walking briskly, as if they owned the street. Their radar is going all the time without their even being aware of it. They learn to have eyes in back of their heads.

It's not an ideal situation, but life is often a trade-off. If you move to a big city you will find it filled with city kids who wouldn't dream of living anywhere else.

Moving to Podunk?

"I'm going to have a hairy fit!" screamed Jessica. "I will never survive moving to a hick town." She struck her chest with her most theatrical gesture. "I can't believe what I'm hearing. You actually expect me to move to the sticks. Why, they've probably never even heard of Benetton out there!"

Her father sighed, and her mother rolled her eyes in despair. They were moving to a beautiful suburban town because a fantastic job had opened up at corporate headquarters.

They, too, loved the city and were not happy to be leaving, but they were seriously worried about Jessica's attitude. If she came on that way to the kids she would be meeting, she was going to have a very bumpy ride.

In one of the college handbooks, cow tipping is described as a major activity of students at a rural college. This is the practice of sneaking up on a cow while it is sleeping and—you guessed it—tipping it over.

Now if you're coming from a town where they deal drugs on one corner and have a great ballet company dancing in a theater on the other corner, that may seem a wee bit tame. But as they say around town, "Don't knock it until you've tried it."

There's a lot to be said for life in the slow lane. Tipping cows may never be your bag, especially if you're used to watching life zoom by at 100 mph, but if you've discovered slow dancing, you know that speed is not one of life's essential ingredients.

Life may move at a slower pace outside a big city, but it is easier to make friends. You can live in a big-city apartment house for years and never know the names of the people down the hall. You may not even know what they look like.

When you move to a small town the Welcome

Wagon lady stops by to say hello and offer maps, general information, and discount coupons from stores and restaurants.

Your neighbors will probably walk over as you're moving in, introduce themselves, and try to make you feel at home. They'll point out the houses that have kids your age and try to arrange for you to meet them.

People in a small town know more about you and what you are doing. That has its advantages and disadvantages. Privacy is a big-city bonus, but then you don't experience the kind of extended family feeling that often develops on a block in the suburbs.

It's comforting to walk down the street and know that the people watching are friendly. It's even better to know that if you're in trouble—whether it's that you forgot your key or just had a fight with your mother— you can knock on a nearby door and someone will let you in.

Before you make friends in school, you make friends with the kids on the block. They often remain your truest friends, the basic support group you turn to as you would to a family.

When you're little you play out in the street with the other kids or hang out in someone's family room on a rainy afternoon. As you grow up you all sit on the front steps together and talk about life.

Five-year-old Mark and his family had just moved from an apartment in Manhattan to a house in a small New Jersey town.

"I love it here, Mom," he said one day. "You remember how in New York you had to take me out every time I wanted to play with someone. Now I can just open the door and walk down the street and find a friend."

Some Like It Hot

Marilyn moved from Ohio to Alaska. The first winter there she thought she would die of the cold.

"I'll never be warm again," she wrote to her best friend, Susan.

Two years later the family decided to spend Christmas in Cleveland visiting Grandma and all their old friends. Marilyn gave Grandma a big kiss and then announced she was going over to Susan's house.

"Do you want a lift?" her father asked.

Marilyn looked out on the snow-covered lawns sparkling in the sun.

"No, thanks," she said. "It's such a beautiful day, I think I'll walk."

She threw a light jacket over her shoulders and happily strolled the few blocks, basking in the unexpected warmth.

Susan opened the door and quickly dragged Marilyn into the house.

"You poor thing!" she exclaimed. "You must be freezing! Let me make you some hot chocolate right away."

You can't stand the cold. Your mother hates the heat. We all feel that if we had to move to an area where the climate was too hot or cold for us, we would be miserable.

The fact is that the body is an adaptable instrument. By the end of her second year in Alaska, Marilyn was not feeling the cold any more than her friends who had grown up there. Had she moved to the tropics, she would have found that after a while the extreme heat ceased to bother her.

We are lucky to be able to adapt physically to new surroundings. If we are also smart, we make the best of them.

When Marilyn realized that she wouldn't turn to ice if she set foot outside, she discovered the pleasure of snow that didn't melt in a few days and the joy of skiing from November to April. Had she moved south, she could have learned to water ski and had the fun of swimming almost every day.

Adapting to a new climate is one of the easiest adjustments to make and can offer unexpected rewards.

They Speak a Different Language

Judy and her family moved from Baltimore to a town in the hills of Tennessee. When she came home after her first day in school, she sat down at the kitchen table and started to bawl.

"What happened, honey?" her mother asked, deeply concerned. "Were the other kids mean to you?"

"No," sobbed Judy, "they were okay."

"Was it the teacher...?"

Judy shook her head.

"For heaven's sake," said her mother, "please stop crying and tell me what happened."

"It's just that...I could hardly understand a word they were saying. Even the teacher. Like they were talking a foreign language."

Our country is so vast that there are still pockets where anyone from outside the area would have a hard time understanding the local dialect. These are generally isolated sections where the people still have limited contact with the "outside world."

This kind of thing is an extreme and becoming increasingly rare, but certainly we are all familiar with regional differences—the Southern drawl, the Western twang, the Brooklyn accent.

Even a mild change in speech can be startling to the ear, but after a while you begin to assimilate and find yourself picking up local speech patterns. When you go back to your old hometown you may find your friends laughing at *your* accent.

The language itself can be different throughout the country. A Coke can be called a soda in New York, a phosphate in New England, and pop in the South. Meanings of words can vary as you move from one local area to another, or sometimes just from town to town.

Liza moved from New York City to Montclair, New Jersey, only fifteen miles away. She had lived there a few weeks when one night at dinner she made a joking remark to her brother and ended it by saying "Sap!"

"That's terribly rude," said her mother. "You apologize right now."

"What for?" asked Liza. "What did I do?"

"You called your brother a sap," replied her mother indignantly.

Liza and her brother both burst out laughing.

"It's not what you think," she explained. "It's kind of a word they use here. It means, sort of a joke."

The Political Scene

Even though you know you should be aware of local and national politics, and that it would probably be a good idea to be involved at some level, chances are it's all a big yawn to you. The heated arguments between your parents and their friends put you to sleep when you were younger, and you still would rather watch "Hill Street Blues." But in spite of yourself, something has rubbed off.

You have a pretty good idea of what political party your parents prefer, how they feel about the current President, the kinds of social programs they would like to see enacted, and so on. You may have grown up in a neighborhood where everyone sounds off with different, very loud opinions. But it's not like that everywhere.

You may have parents who never discuss politics with you. You may have grown up in a neighborhood where everybody feels pretty much the same way about the role of government and the people who should govern.

If you move from one kind of atmosphere to the other, you may find yourself very upset. Understandably so. You may feel you will never fit in because your views (or your family's) are so different from those you find around you now. That's okay.

The world is big enough for everyone to think his or her own thoughts and to express them. Any thoughtful opinion, expressed honestly and openly, is usually listened to.

Most people respect your right to say and believe what you want, even if they don't agree with you. And if you find your opinions are not respected or listened to, ask yourself, "Do I want this person as my friend?"

Moving Up?

Roger gaped at the cars in the high school parking lot. He had never seen such a collection. BMWs and Porsches were sprinkled liberally among the shiny new Corvettes and Chrysler convertibles.

He had been so excited when Dad told him that sixteen was the driving age in the state they were moving to and the new job would enable him to get Roger a car.

"Maybe it will take some of the sting out of leaving all your friends," Dad had explained.

Driving out of the used-car lot in his very own white VW rabbit had been the biggest thrill of Roger's life. But the thrill was dissipating rapidly as he swung into the parking space next to a bright red 'Vette.

"This kind of stuff is way over my head," Roger thought as he made his way to class feeling smaller and less important every minute.

Or Moving Down?

Mary Jane could hardly contain her disappointment when she saw her new house. It wasn't that they had moved from a mansion or anything like one.

They had been living in a neat white Cape Cod with a small lawn in the front and a swing set in the back. The main difference between their house and all the other Cape Cods on the street was that their shutters were pink.

But their new house was so small and dreary. The room she used to share with her sister had not been large, but when they put their twin beds in the new room, there was hardly any space to walk around.

And the house was this dull green, and if you stuck your hand out the window you could practically touch the house next door, and there was hardly any lawn and only one spindly tree out front...

"I just don't get it," she complained to her parents. "We got $150,000 for our old house. That's a lot of money! Why couldn't we get another one just as nice."

"That's a good question, honey," said her father with a sigh. "Unfortunately, when you move from one state to another, prices for houses change. And this is what $150,000 looks like here."

Balancing the Scale

Some of us are lucky. We move to more of the same scene, and it's almost as if we never left home. For most of us, however, moving means a different kind of neighborbood and a different social scene than the one we are used to.

If we are moving "up," it's easy to feel more than a bit uncomfortable among kids who seem to take for granted material possessions that are very special to us. They are used to the large house and the shiny new car. It's no big deal to them. It shouldn't be a big deal to us either.

Roger doesn't change because his father now has more money. Even if Dad were now getting twice his new salary, he would never have dreamed of buying Roger an expensive sports car.

"No way!" he would have said. "Not for a kid. This is IT until you start earning your own money. Then, my boy, the sky's the limit."

A BMW doesn't make a fellow student better than you. It doesn't make him worse either. It is a meaningless symbol, but we are inclined to invest it with importance.

If we are moving "down," it's easy to feel sad about what used to be and to think that nothing new can compare to what we once had.

Mary Jane wasn't a snob, but the more nostalgic she became about the way things once were, the more dissatisfied she became with everything about her now. And, of course, her attitude showed.

"Who does she think she is?" commented the girl next door. "Princess Di?"

It's important to remember that moving up or down has nothing to do with us. It doesn't make us better or worse. Roger and Mary Jane haven't changed, but they have to stop looking up or down at everyone. They have to learn to balance the scale by holding on to their own values, regardless of the world around them.

100% American

Unless your ancestors were Native Americans, they like everyone else in this country came over on a boat—even if that boat was called the *Mayflower*. We are all immigrants. Most of us couldn't speak English when we arrived and when we finally did learn the language, we had the funniest accent...

And yet there are people who believe some immigrants are better than other immigrants because of the country they came from and when they came here. This is called prejudice.

If you have not met up with it, you have indeed been fortunate, but when you move, that demon may enter your life. Be prepared to face it.

Prejudice causes people to dislike you before they even meet you. It has many faces. Your religion, the color of your skin, the country you or your family came from, is all prejudiced people need to know about you. And all they want to know.

People who have met with discrimination know what to expect, but if you are coming from a protected environment, your first dose of prejudice can be shattering.

The high school Steve used to attend had students of many different backgrounds, colors, and faiths. You were accepted or rejected because of the kind of person you were, not because of an accident of birth. Although Steve was black, his world was color-blind.

When he moved, he was one of three black students in his new school. The fact that the school was almost entirely white registered with Steve, but simply as a fact, not as a matter of concern. What did concern him was the difficulty he was having in making friends.

Maybe it's my clothes, he thought. Or maybe they expect me to make the overtures.

At lunch the next day he went over to a boy in his Math class.

"Hi," he said, sticking out his hand, "I'm Steve Gordon. I'm in Algebra 103 with you and I was wondering if you took down today's assignment."

"It's still on the board if you want it," said the boy,

ignoring Steve's outstretched hand and turning back to his tablemates.

As Steve, more puzzled than hurt, was leaving the lunchroom, one of the kids from a nearby table came over to him.

"I saw what happened just now," he commiserated. "Don't let that dip get to you. We're not all like that."

There is a very moving song in the musical *South Pacific* concerning prejudice. "You have to be taught to hate. . ." is its theme.

Babies aren't born with a belief that some religions, or colors of skin, or shapes of eyes are better than others. They are taught prejudice by unthinking people. And unless someone opens their eyes, they don't think any further than their parents did. But if you are at the receiving end of their ignorance, it can hurt. A lot.

You can deal with prejudice by ignoring it, arguing about it, or striking back. Only you can decide the best way for you to react.

Many people deal with prejudice by ignoring it. They feel that nothing will come of debating the point or trying to convince a narrow-minded person of the truth. They turn away because they don't want a confrontation. They can shrug it off for what it is—ignorance and stupidity.

Some people react physically to the insult. Their response is to punch the other guy in the mouth and walk away feeling better. Since the other guy usually hits back, this approach can be rather complicated.

Other people have to express their feelings in words.

They want to argue the point. Even if they can't change someone's mind, they feel better for trying.

You owe nothing to prejudice. It's a nasty thing, and if you are forced to deal with it, you should do it in a way you feel is best for you.

Fortunately, prejudice is no longer fashionable. There was a time when many people openly expressed biased views. This is increasingly rare. Although you may meet with it in a new environment, you will probably find, as Steve did, that the prejudiced person is the exception, not the rule.

Chapter XI

Your New Friends

Diana sighed as she watched the tall blond with the crew cut amble across the room and slouch behind his desk.

"I'd give up my tickets to the next Genesis concert if I could get to meet him," she whispered to the girl next to her.

"What's your problem?" asked her friend. "Just go over after class and tell him you're having a party Friday night and would he like to come."

"I couldn't do that!" protested Diana. "Girls just don't go up to boys they don't even know and ask them to a party."

"Maybe they don't in Squeedunk, but they sure do here. Don't tell me you're going to sit around hoping someone will ask you out. You'll never get a guy that way!"

"Join a fraternity?" roared Jeff. "Not on your life! I think the whole Greek system stinks, and I don't want any part of it."

His new friend, Bob, shrugged. "Nobody's saying the system is perfect, but it has its good points. And just try getting a date on a Saturday night if you can't take the girl to a frat party. It's the only fun thing to do in this burg."

Susan looked impatiently at her watch. Only five minutes had passed. It seemed like an hour. She couldn't take it any more. She picked up the phone.

"Hi, Bill," she said. "I was just wondering what time you were thinking of coming over."

"Oh yeah," Bill replied. "I was meaning to call you. Some of the guys want to go bowling tonight and I kind of promised I'd go with them. We'll make it another night. Okay?"

Susan hung up, stunned. How could he do this to her? He hadn't exactly asked her to go out, but he had asked if she was doing anything and said he would call. How could he leave her dangling and then casually dismiss her? What kind of a boy was he?

"Very macho," said her friend Barbara the next day. "That's the way all the guys are around here. You'd better get used to it."

Social Security

The way males and females relate to each other varies sharply from one part of the country to another. In some areas a girl is expected to be submissive, to wait for a boy to call, to understand if he doesn't, to take the crumbs and be happy they're offered.

Susan has a difficult choice. She can demand respect, but she will have a hard time finding it in a town where boys grow up believing that men call the shots and women should be there when they're wanted. In the meantime, the girls who are less demanding will be partying—when they're asked.

In other areas boys ask girls for dates, but they also expect to be asked out. A girl will call and suggest a movie just as easily as a boy will. And when they go, they pay their own way.

Diane managed to meet her tall blond hero by changing her seat in class—a complicated process that definitely involved the Genesis tickets. Once they had met, however, she found it was not all that difficult to create a Friday night party and casually ask him if he'd like to drop by.

Sororities and fraternities are major factors in some high schools and virtually unknown in others. Joining or not joining is an individual decision.

Many people disapprove of the Greek system because they feel it breeds snobbishness and causes unnecessary hurt. On the other hand, those who belong speak of the unusual closeness and long-term friendships that are often formed.

And of course—there are those wild parties...

Peer Pressure

Speak to a hundred teenagers in a hundred parts of the country and they will all agree—there is no such thing as peer pressure.

"Nobody puts pressure on me to smoke grass," says Naomi. "I only do it at parties when someone offers me a joint. But I can take it or leave it. Nobody is going to make fun of me if I don't smoke. I do it because it's fun once in a while."

"Sure I drink beer," says Gerald. "I know I'm underage and the cops would bust me if they caught me, but what's the big fuss about a six-pack among friends. Look, nobody makes me drink. I do it because I want to."

"Grow up," says Marie. "How many girls do you think are still virgins when they get out of high school? And how many of those are virgins because nobody asked them? Nobody forces you to do it. Sure, guys ask. You can always say no."

Does peer pressure exist? Of course it does. We may not choose to recognize it. We can tell ourselves we drink or do drugs or have sex only because we want to, not because we would feel uncomfortable in the crowd if we backed off. We can succumb to the pressure and pretend it's not there, but it's not smart to fool yourself.

Subtle, unspoken pressures exist at every level. You were used to the pressures that were part of your growing up, and you learned to deal with them. You knew how far you wanted to go and when you wanted to walk away.

When you move, the rules change. The pressures are there, but they're not exactly the same as the ones you knew before. They're harder to recognize and therefore harder to cope with.

Learning the Ropes

Rose came from a blue-collar town where kids worked after school to earn money for movies, tapes, or a slice of pizza. Nobody handed them anything.

Almost nobody did drugs because almost nobody had the money to buy them.

When she moved, Rose went to the regional high school that covered a number of towns, blue-collar to upper-middle. A lot of the kids had a lot of money to spend.

Smoking pot was a given. There was always a keg or two at parties, and it was rumored that once or twice someone had sprinkled cocaine on the popcorn. Just good clean fun!

Rose enjoyed her new friends. They were a lot livelier than those she had left behind. She began to press for a later curfew.

"Everybody else can stay out until one on Saturday. Why do I have to be home so early?"

"And since when are you everybody else?" demanded her mother. "Just because you've met a bunch of kids whose parents seem to have more money than brains doesn't mean we're not going to be responsible parents any more.

"We make rules we feel are right for you at this age. I can't worry about what every other kid does. That's a job for their parents."

It was easy for Rose to fall in with the new crowd. She wanted to make friends—and how attractive they seemed. But she was lucky. Her parents had not left their values behind when they moved, and they helped her find hers again.

It can be hard to hold fast to your own identity when you leave behind all that is familiar and comfortable and try to move into a world you don't know. You want to make friends, and the temptation to latch on to the first person who reaches out to you is enormous.

Of course you want to respond to friendship when it is offered, but try not to lose your balance. Ask yourself a few searching questions and answer them privately—but honestly.

Do I really like this person or am I just feeling lonely?

Do I want this person as a friend, or really more as someone who can open doors to a larger group?

Do I have the same values as my new friends, or am I trying to adapt to theirs?

Do I know who I am and where I am coming from, or am I losing sight of my own identity and values?

Be Yourself

One of the hidden benefits of moving is that you are usually forced to ask yourself, "Who am I?" Most kids never have the need to ask that question. They just go with the flow.

Now you have to choose the flow you will go with. It can be a problem. It can cause you a lot of anxiety. But the answers you find can be one of the best things you'll ever do for yourself.

Chapter **XII**

The Heat Is On Again

In a musical called *Wonderful Town* that was popular when Mother was a girl, two sisters come to New York from a small town in Ohio. They find an apartment in Greenwich Village—and problems beyond their wildest dreams. Among them is the building of a subway right under their feet.

Just as they think they have made it through their first traumatic day in the Big Apple, there is an underground blast that knocks out their lights and rattles every dish, cup, and window.

Clutching each other in sheer panic, the two sisters wail: "Why, Oh why, Oh why-O. Why did we ever leave Ohio?"

At some point, everyone who has ever left home—either by choice or by chance—wishes they hadn't. There is no age limit on being homesick. It can happen to you. It can happen to your father and mother. And it probably will—to all of you. What do you do about it? You can't go home again, so how do you adjust to the present reality?

Bothered and Bewildered

The worst is over. You lived through that unique torture called moving. You're into your second week in school, and you no longer feel as if you have a social disease every time you walk into the lunchroom.

So why have you suddenly broken out with zits so humongous that your face looks like the surface of the moon?

And why is your sister climbing the wall with menstrual cramps when her previous periods were so casual she used to worry about being taken unawares?

Watch out! That old devil, stress, is tapping on your shoulder again.

You thought you were under a lot of stress before you moved—and you were, but at least you were on familiar turf. Now you and the family are trying to cope with a new town, new schools or jobs, new friends. And besides, you are homesick. You miss the friends and family you left behind.

Now you know what stress really is!

You may not feel it the moment you move in. It may not show up for a week or two, or more. But don't be surprised when it does.

This time, however, you have some weapons you didn't have before:

1. You can recognize the symptoms of stress. They may not be the same as those you experienced before you moved, but it doesn't take too much detective work to figure out that the lack of appetite, or the need to gorge on Rocky Road ice cream, or the face full of zits, or the extraordinary cramps are clear signs of stress.

2. You know you're not alone. You know that everyone in your family is feeling the same kind of anxiety, whether it is open or hidden. You're all in the same boat.

3. This time you know there is something you can do about it. You know that talking with each other helps. It's not quite so hard to keep from killing your kid brother if you know that at least some of his impossible behavior stems from stress he is feeling.

Symptom Watch

Forewarned is forearmed. If you know you may have a strong emotional or physical reaction to moving, you are halfway toward self-help. You can be on the lookout for excessive reactions:

Are you often very very angry, very very quickly?
Are you tired all the time?
Does life seem a big bore even though you're busier than you ever have been?
Have you lost your appetite?
Are you eating two or three times as much as usual?
Do you get stomachaches, headaches, excessive cramps?
Is your acne much more noticeable?
Have you started to bite your nails again?
You name it...

It helps to understand that all these things may be symptoms of the stress that comes with moving into a new environment, that it is only natural to react that way, and that the symptoms will probably begin to disappear as you feel more at home in your new home.

A Family Affair

Just as you can be on the lookout for symptoms of stress in yourself, you can more easily recognize them in the rest of your family. And you can be sure they will be there.

So what? Who said it was your role to do anything about it?

You did. In your heart you have to know that if you are more aware of a problem—and what to do about it—than anyone else in the family, your knowledge carries responsibility with it.

Okay. Granted you'd like to do something. How can you help?

The greatest gift we have to give each other as human beings is sympathetic communication. In other words, we can talk to each other with our hearts.

If your family eats dinner together, then the dinner table is a ready-made forum. If you don't have any regular time to get together, suggest one. Call a meeting for Sunday afternoon or another convenient time. And then begin to talk to each other.

You can start it off.

"I feel awful and I need to talk about it. I feel like crying all the time. I don't think I'll ever make any friends, and classes are so tough here and..."

Once you start talking, it will be like opening the floodgates. You won't be able to stop, and you'll begin to feel better just by expressing your feelings, airing your own troubles.

You will probably be surprised at the sensitivity of the playback. That impossible kid brother may have some amazing insights into the way you feel—and even some helpful suggestions.

Once you lead the way, the rest of the family will find it easier to talk about their problems, needs, anxieties, hopes, and fears. As you listen to each other talk, you will find you will all be more patient and understanding.

You can become a support group for each other during this difficult time. Whether the conversations begins with informal talk around the dinner table, or whether you have to set a specific time to get together, you will find the meetings helpful.

You can start your second meeting by asking questions that show you were paying attention the first time around.

"Did you find someone to have lunch with?"

"Is biology getting any better, or do you think you should get a tutor?"

"Do you think the manager of the shipping department likes you any better now that he sees you're not a threat to his job?"

Et cetera.

Each of you will benefit by being able to express his or her feelings openly to people who care. It helps not only to talk, but to know that you are being listened to with a sympathetic ear.

There is an old saying: "If you get stuck with a bushel of lemons, make lemonade."

Making the best of a situation you can't change is one of the hallmarks of growing up. Talking to your family to relieve the stress caused by moving is like making lemonade out of excess lemons. It will help all of you cope better with the immediate problems, but it will undoubtedly have even broader effects.

When you work together as a family on a common problem, the bonds grow stronger and the feelings deeper. The theme is: We're all in this together. We can talk it through. We can give to each other—and make each one of us the richer for the experience of giving.

Chapter **XIII**

Finding Friends

It was still dark when the alarm clock went off, but Lila was used to that. If she was going to run her three miles before school today, she had to be up with the birds.

Sleepily she pulled herself out of bed. It was always such a temptation to go back to sleep, but she made herself think about the weight she had lost and how great she felt after running. It was a real high, and it set her up to face the day.

She would certainly need all the help she could get facing this day, she thought as she laced her shoes snugly. The first day of school was traditionally hard, but there had always been familiar faces in class. Today she wouldn't know a single soul.

One of the good things about her new house was that it was only a few blocks from a large park. She jogged over to the entrance and started down the path that circled the ball fields. As she rounded the first turn she heard the familiar sound of another runner coming toward her. She looked up.

He was gorgeous. He was built. He was worth getting up for. They nodded at each other as they passed.

At the other end of the oval they passed each other again. This time he smiled. Her pulse rate doubled.

The next time they met he waved. And smiled. Her pulse rate tripled. As she came out of the park there he was, running in place waiting for the traffic to pass. "It was great this morning, wasn't it," he said. Lila nodded, out of breath. "Maybe I'll see you tomorrow," he called back over his shoulder. Maybe? thought Lila, as she floated home. The only maybe is if I break both legs—and even then I'll find a way...

Skills Transfer

Whether you're a jogger, a skier, a musician, or an actor, the skills and interests you have developed are always with you. When you move, those skills become more than just a hobby or a sport. They can be your passport to finding friends in a new world.

When you're looking for friends, you can't mount a street-corner soapbox, or grab interesting-looking people as they rush past you in the halls between classes, but it's easy to make friends when you have something in common.

You are at your best when you are doing something you enjoy. You feel comfortable, so it is easier for you to be outgoing. Talking to a stranger seems more natural if you start off sharing an activity. What happens after you start talking is up to you.

Whatever your skill, find out who's doing what about it? Is there an amateur theater group, a ski club, a town-wide baseball league? Ask around. Look in the local paper. Check the bulletin board at the supermarket. Find out what's happening and when.

Also remember, you don't have to be a champion to go for it. Your skills may be limited, but if your interest is high you'll enjoy just being a part of the group, and your enthusiasm will help win you a place in it—even if you can't make it on talent alone.

Maybe you were never a joiner. You never needed to be one. You grew up knowing everyone in town anyhow. After school you and your friends would just hang out. That was the big activity. Well, now you can't just go and hang out because you don't know where to hang out and you don't have anyone to hang out with.

One of the best ways to make new friends is to join a club or other organization, but make sure it is an activity you enjoy. Don't join a group just to meet people. Join for the fun of it, and the friends will follow.

School Activities

Most high school have more clubs, teams, and other groups than students. If sports is your bag, go out for the team your first day of school.

Talk to the coach. Find out when tryouts are and let him know you'd like a shot at it. Try to latch on to a schedule of games so you can plan your schedule ahead.

If you're the kind who likes to lie down until the urge for physical activity passes, check out the club scene. Most schools have a handbook that lists all the clubs and their advisers. If there's no handbook, central office probably has some kind of list.

If chess intrigues you, if you'd like to get more practice in a foreign language, if you're looking for fellow camera buffs, you can probably find students who share your interest. If you have no special hobby, you might like to join something like the Hospitality Club that provides hosts and hostesses for school events.

Maybe you'd like to go out for the school paper, but think you don't have enough talent. If you're good at writing, so much the better, but you don't have to be Shakespeare to work on production or solicit ads.

And as everywhere else in life, there's always politics—the general school organization, the school council, class office—any of these will get you into the swing of things quickly and provide some valuable life experiences.

Community Activities

Every community is filled with social, religious, political, and service groups. Some are primarily for adults, but many either encourage teenage participation or are geared to young adults.

Religious groups are everywhere. Churches and temples always sponsor youth groups and go out of their way to seek out newcomers to the community. You will be sure of finding a warm welcome. It is one way to begin to feel at home right away.

Local political clubs are also interested in finding young people who are willing to get involved. They are particularly active—and particularly in need of help—during the few months before local or national elections.

Even though you can't vote, you can help them turn out the vote, a vital activity in our democracy, and a fascinating one to be a part of.

Boy Scouts, Girl Scouts, and 4-H are, of course, among the most active teenage community groups. If you were a member previously, there is an immediate bond and you know you will be accepted readily. If you have never been a member, these are wonderful groups to learn more about because their activities are so broad.

Work Your Way Up

Volunteer work is emotionally rewarding and is another way to meet people. Most communities have youth programs—drug rehab, alcohol abuse prevention, and, unfortunately, suicide watch. It's not fun and games, but if helping others makes *you* feel good, it's a great way to help yourself as well.

Hospitals also need teenage volunteers. Their needs vary, as do their age requirements, but becoming a candy striper is a special kind of benefit—again, to yourself, as much as to others.

Getting a job after school can bring friends along with pocket money. But play it smart. Try to land a job where there's some teenage action—McDonald's, Dunkin Donuts, Carvel, or Dairy Queen...

Behind the Scenes

Martha loved to sing. She joined the church choir. She joined the school chorus. She joined the local operetta club.

She met a lot of nice older folks in the church choir. She met a lot of nice girls in the chorus. She met a lot of nice middle-aged amateur singers in the operetta club.

Martha was new in town. It was pleasant to be meeting a lot of other girls and a lot of nice older people. It would have been even more pleasant if at least one of them were a seventeen-year-old baritone, but Martha shrugged it off. She was there because she *loved* to sing, not to find a boyfriend.

But guess what?

One of the nice old ladies in the church choir had a grandson who was into Tchaikovsky *and* Talking Heads.

One of the nice girls in the chorus had a brother who was the most promising junior on the football team and who liked to sing in the shower.

None of the nice middle-aged hams in the operetta club were related to any teenage boys, but about five guys from the high school always built sets, painted scenery, and worked lights for each production.

And the moral is, of course...

Do what you enjoy doing. Certainly become involved, but choose something you want to do—not something you think you should do because it seems to be a better way to meet people.

When you're involved with something you enjoy, you're more YOU. You're relaxed. You're thinking about what you're doing, not what other people will think of you. And it makes you all the more attractive so that the nice old lady will think about introducing you to her grandson.

Don't Just Sit There

You can spend every afternoon and evening at a different club and still make very few new friends. You have to become involved. You have to participate. You can't just sit there.

If you join a club, sign up for a committee right away. It will give you the opportunity to meet people in small groups, to talk to them one on one, to work on a project together—and for them to get to know you.

If you go out for a sport, go all the way.

You love to swim? Great. You can join the Y and swim laps until your hips are two inches smaller, but that alone will not necessarily help you make friends. Use your skills and talents to the fullest. Take a course in lifesaving. Breaking holds is a great icebreaker. It's impossible to remain aloof when someone is trying to drown you.

And what about CPR? Whom would *you* like to practice on? It's not against the rules to look around before you pick a partner.

Make your own fun. You don't have to sit around and wait to be discovered. Throw a "We've Just Moved In Don't Mind The Mess" party.

By now you've met a few people. Invite them over and ask them to invite the five or ten most interesting people they know.

Big Shot

Betty moved from New York City—THE Big Apple

—to a small town in Indiana. Kicking and screaming all the way.

"They're all just a bunch of dumb hicks," she announced to her parents after one only day in school. "I'm going to die of boredom here."

Each time she met someone new, Betty made it very clear that leaving New York was a tragedy and how sorry she felt for anyone who had to be stuck in "a dumb hick town like this one."

Betty could not understand why she wasn't able to make any friends. "I guess I'm just too smart for them," she told her parents bitterly.

Chameleon

A chameleon, as you may remember from General Science, is a small lizard that takes its color from the nearest object and changes color as it moves. Fascinating in the world of reptiles, but not a big plus in human beings. Like Brian.

Brian felt so alone and was so eager to make friends that he would follow them anywhere. If someone suggested picking up a couple of six-packs with a false ID, Brian would be right behind him—knees shaking, hands sweating, but right there nevertheless.

He never had an opinion of his own. If Jack said the football team was the worst one ever created, Brian would agree. If Bill said the football team may have lost a few tough ones but would surely come out on top in the long run, Brian would nod sympathetically. There was as many Brians as there were people he met up with. No one could ever be a good friend to Brian because no one person could ever know him.

Be Yourself

Friends are people who know us well—and *still* like us! We make friends by being ourselves, by letting it all hang out. But you don't have to shoot off your mouth the moment you meet someone. When you move to a new area, there are new ground rules to learn. You don't have to change what you are to suit the rules, but it's helpful to know them. Listen to what people say, listen to the way they talk. You don't have to be a Brian and go along mindlessly agreeing with everyone, but you don't have to go out of your way to antagonize everyone.

If you're a strong person and feel good about yourself—and you will always like yourself better when you are true to YOU—you can afford to take the time to understand what makes this new world tick. Then you can choose the way you want to function in it and whom *you* want as your new friends.

Chapter XIV

Great Adventure

Moving is what you make it.

You can feel sorry for yourself and indulge in the "Why me" syndrome. You can bob along like the cork on the ocean, not planning ahead, just letting it happen and ending up wherever the tide takes you.

Or you can look at moving as an exciting challenge. Something is changing in your life. You can take control and try to make the transition as smooth as possible. You can face reality and approach the change with a positive attitude. You can make it a great adventure!

When Bob moved to Manhattan, the first thing he did was buy a guidebook. The second thing was to start walking.

Bob already knew many places he wanted to visit—the Statue of Liberty, the Metropolitan Museum of Art, the top of the Empire State Building. Dozens of other wonderful, exciting "sights." And like any tourist, he saw most of them.

But Bob was more than a tourist. Now he was a New Yorker. He wanted to learn what his hometown was really like, so he began walking.

He discovered that New York was a city full of small

neighborhoods. Almost every nationality he had ever heard of was represented. The shops, the restaurants, and best of all—the bakeries—varied from one area to the next.

He began to tell some of his new friends in school about his discoveries. They had lived in New York all their lives, but they didn't know there was a great Hungarian (or German, or Italian, or Polish) bakery only ten blocks away. Would Bob mind if they came along the next time he went walking?

"This is a nice enough town, but it sure is dull. Nothing ever happens here. There's no place to go, and nothing to see."

Marta heard the same words over and over, every time she met someone new and asked about Rockside.

"It's a nice place to live," was the standard crack, "but I sure wouldn't want to visit."

Marta couldn't believe that her new home could really be as dull as everyone said.

"Go to the library," her mother suggested. "If there's anything special about Rockside, they'll know."

"Rockside is *full* of history and adventure," said the librarian. "Why, do you know that the Battle of Rockside changed the course of the American Revolution?"

With that she pulled out several oversized books and showed Marta how the British advance had been stopped by the wall of rock that formed the western border of the town.

"We were able to bring our forces up here," said the librarian, pointing to the top of the cliff, "because our soldiers knew about a hidden path. They dragged a couple of cannons up with them and—bam! It was like shooting ducks in a pond. The British finally turned tail and went back to the coast—and ran smack into General Washington!"

The librarian showed Marta some old maps of the town. Marta was fascinated.

"What a great idea for my term paper," she concluded.

A few months later the paper was finished, and her American History teacher asked Marta to talk to the class about it.

"Everybody keeps telling me what a dull town this is," Marta began. "Dull town, indeed," she continued. "What's so dull about changing the course of the American Revolution?"

The class was intrigued. All of them had heard tales about the glorious Battle of Rockside, but none of them had ever taken the trouble to investigate it further.

But Marta went that extra mile and came up with a treasure—not in gold, but in the excitement her story created among her new friends in their town—and in her.

"Why me? Why do I have to have all the bad luck?"

Throw yourself a Pity Party and blame everything that happens on bad luck. Or take a positive stand and face the things that can't be changed with a smile.

Luck certainly plays a part in what happens to each of us in this world, but generally only a small part. Life does not depend on a roll of the dice. It depends on how we look at the world.

The world is not made up of daydreams and

chocolate bars. It is made up of reality. Luck is what we make it. There *is* a pony somewhere—if you want to look for it.

For most of us, moving is a time of anxiety, stress, and often sadness. But a new beginning *can* be wonderful. Exploring a new town or city, meeting people who would never have come into your life otherwise, broadening your horizons—all this is part of coping with moving and with growing up.

Moving is an ending. We move from one life to another, but we have learn that life is full of endings. What counts is the way we deal with the endings.

It has been said that the basic function of a family is to help children develop roots *and* wings. Your experience with this move can help you develop your wings and give you some of the confidence in yourself that you will need when the time comes to try them out.

Index